MANAGING THE MODERN ECONOMY

MANAGING THE MODERN ECONOMY

A Short Handbook Of
The New Economics

Jan S. Hogendorn
COLBY COLLEGE and BOĞAZİÇİ ÜNİVERSİTESİ

WINTHROP PUBLISHERS, INC.,
Cambridge, Massachusetts

Cover by Steve Snider

CONTENTS

PREFACE

Economics is not the easiest of subjects. In the last three decades, burgeoning theoretical studies have made even introductory economics books large tomes of 800 pages or more, while an ever more mathematical approach has meant a steady increase in complexity and greater demands on the reader.

This book is different. It is short, lighter in style than most introductory books in economics, and it attempts to hold analysis to the required minimum.

Its subject matter is modern economic policy in theory and practice— "Keynesian macroeconomics" to the initiated, or the "New Economics," to use the more popular terminology. Basically, the book examines how policy is used to maintain economic stability—the avoidance of depressions and inflations. In passing it develops the tools needed to understand policy decisions, points out the pitfalls in economic management which are so apparent to Americans experiencing the uncertain economic conditions of the early 1970's, and concludes with a full analysis of the dramatic emergency measures instituted by the Nixon Administration in August, and December 1971.

All this is done much more comprehensively in the famous textbooks on economic principles used in first-year college courses, among the most noteworthy being Paul A. Samuelson's *Economics*, McGraw-Hill, New York, 8th edition, 1970, from an earlier edition of which the author learned his first economics. Less advanced analysis and thus greater ease of assimilation can be found in Campbell McConnell, *Economics*, McGraw-Hill, New York, 1969. Also well-written, but at a higher level, is Richard G. Lipsey and Peter O. Steiner, *Economics*, 2nd edition, Harper and Row, New York, 1969.

However, all these texts share the difficulty of being rather heavy going and lengthy. There appears to be a place for a narrative treatment of modern economic policy which, as noted earlier, covers the essentials, but is kept short. Several uses are foreseen for this little volume: college students in regular economics courses should find it a compact method for reviewing the material in a standard text, or it could be used on its own for "short courses" in colleges and junior colleges, and also in some high schools.

Perhaps even more important, it is hoped that the book will give an introduction to economic policy-making which reaches readers who would not ordinarily want to work their way through a full-size text. Students of sociology, political science, business, history, and law all need some understanding of this area. Furthermore, businessmen, people active in government, and concerned voters might well appreciate a readable approach to the subject. The concluding chapters should be especially welcome to all groups of readers as they cover the important new economic policy decisions of August and December 1971.

The content of the book owes much to the texts of Samuelson, McConnell, and Lipsey and Steiner and to Professor Lipsey himself, with whom the author studied advanced topics in macroeconomics in Lipsey's Seminar at the London School of Economics. Its particular framework took shape during a series of television lectures given on Maine Educational TV in 1969.

Thanks are due to Winthrop Publishers for their assistance, to Colby College for a grant to cover the expenses of preparation, and to the various readers of the manuscript who provided many helpful criticisms. Any errors remaining are of course the author's, although to vary a familiar theme, it is a shame that they were not caught by the friends who read the draft copies.

Jan S. Hogendorn
Istanbul, Turkey
January 5, 1972

*To S.T.F.
and S.B.
Floreant*

MANAGING THE MODERN ECONOMY

1.

A
FAILURE
OF THE
OLD
ECONOMICS

The following chapters explore the area of modern economic policy-making, sometimes called the "New Economics." This topic forms one of the most important areas of political and academic debate to be found in America today, but is, at the same time, one of the least understood.

HISTORICAL PERSPECTIVE

Why the term "New Economics"? Certainly not because the subject lacks an historical tradition. It dates from at least as early as Professor Adam Smith's famous book, *The Wealth of Nations*, published in our independence year, 1776.[1]

Smith (1723–1790), a lucid writer and brilliant professor (of "Moral Philosophy," as economics was once labeled) at the University of Glasgow in Scotland, has been called the founder of the subject as we know it. Friend of William Pitt, Dr. Samuel Johnson and Boswell, known to Voltaire, Adam Smith

---

[1] *The book is written in an immortal prose style, and every educated person should make a stab at it. It is most accessible in the Modern Library edition (Random House, 1937).*

had an impact on economics which has lasted for the better part of two centuries.[2]

But his great influence was a time bomb in one sense, for Smith in *The Wealth of Nations* concentrated in very large measure on questions which came to be known as "classical," because of the continued attention given them by his followers after 1776 and well into the twentieth century.

The two great classical interrogatives were, first, "Can a society where each person seeks his own selfish ends work for the general good?"[3] and second, "Will an economy continue to grow in size or will it tend to slow down to a stationary state, so-called, where growth ceases?"[4] This led the classical economists to such further inquiries as what determines a market price, both for goods and for items used in production, the need for international trade, the advantages of a division of labor and many more.

The time bomb lay in Smith's tendency to place little emphasis upon the topics which seem crucial today and which are at the heart of the New Economics—depression and inflation, income levels and unemployment.[5] Do not underestimate the classical economists, by the way. They did not ignore these issues, and in fact provided plausible explanations as to why they would not be a serious problem for a nation.[6]

The result was that for most of its history, economics overlooked to a remarkable extent the study of depression, inflation, and unemployment, and all during that long era when the famous writer Thomas Carlyle christened the subject "The Dismal Science" (to the perpetual embarrassment of writers and teachers of the subject), much too little was said on these critical issues.

---

[2]See chapter 3 of Robert L. Heilbroner, The Worldly Philosophers (New York: Simon and Schuster, 3rd edition, 1967) for many anecdotes on the life and times of Adam Smith.

[3]Developed by Smith into the famous theory of the "Invisible Hand."

[4]The most well-known exponent of the stationary state was John Stuart Mill, known to many for his philosophical works such as On Liberty, but who was also a great economist. The theory of the stationary state is found in Mill's Principles of Political Economy (New York: Longmans, Green & Co., 1909). The suggestion contained there is that as more and more economic resources are poured into building factories, machines, houses, etc., this activity becomes less profitable to people undertaking the projects because the most lucrative opportunities are the first to be exhausted. Thus, over a long period of time, such activity might tend to decline greatly.

[5]All of these terms will be more fully defined in due course.

[6]Their classical theories are discussed in the appendix to Chapter 6.

AMERICA: BOOM AND BUST

What happened to change this long neglect of the problems of economic stability?

The roots of the answer lie in the simple, all too obvious fact that the historical record of unfettered capitalism was just not satisfactory. This record shows that America (and many a foreign country as well) has until recently been a land of aptly termed boom and bust cycles in the economy, with depressions in economic activity following inflationary price movements in a seemingly never-ending progression. The truth of this may not always be obvious in an era when economic history is not often taught in our schools or even colleges. To prove the contention that booms and slumps have recurred regularly in our economy, let us highlight some of the important ones in chronological order.[7]

Even before the US Constitution was ratified, the United States had already undergone one of her worst inflations. Due to financial mismanagement, prices rose by a multiple of about 200 in the six years before 1781. Wheat sold at over $100 a bushel that year. Iron prices doubled in a one-month period, and paper currency lost its value to such an extent that a new phrase was born, "Not worth a Continental."

As was invariably true in the classical era of economics, a serious inflation was followed by a period of depression.

These bad times of the 1780's, after a period of recovery, were succeeded by a particularly sharp slump in 1808 caused by Thomas Jefferson's embargo against trading with Europe. This policy was supposed to penalize both Britain and France, but was so harmful to this country that in New England it was called the O-Grab-Me policy (embargo spelled backward). It resulted in ruin for several seaports in the northeast—from which they never fully recovered.[8]

Less than twenty years later there occurred the Panic or Depression of 1837–1841, which historians have termed one of the most dismal periods of our country's history. Business,

---

[7]There are many economic histories of the United States. Most of the details recounted here are embellished upon in Gilbert Fite and Jim Reese, An Economic History of the United States (Boston: Houghton Mifflin Co., 2nd Edition, 1965) and in other texts as well.
[8]For example, Newburyport, Mass., and New Haven, Conn.

manufacturing, and shipping all stagnated and this slump was in fact a great contributor to the western movement as the unemployed sought farms on the frontier.

The great Civil War inflation, bad enough in the north but far worse in the states of the southern Confederacy, was followed in its turn by a severe depression beginning in 1873, one of the longest in our history, with recovery delayed until about 1880. Following revival depression recurred from 1893 to about 1898, when, shades of Dr. Ralph Abernathy, there was a prototype poor people's march on Washington, this one led by an Ohio quarry owner and self-styled general, Jacob Coxey. Coxey's army brought fears of radical action, resulted in the calling out of federal troops and brought disorder to the capitol (all again with a modern ring). It did not match in violence the fusillades of gunfire traded by forces of management and strikers at the Carnegie Steel Company plant at Homestead, Pennsylvania—a result of the company's attempts to reduce the wages of its labor force during this period.

Figure 1–1 shows our experience since 1900. Slumps followed booms with regularity: 1907, 1918–19, the early

Figure 1-1
Business Scale Volume

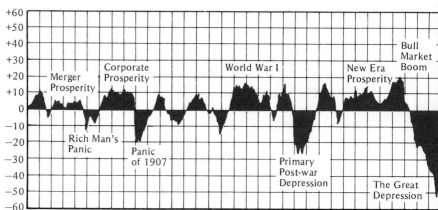

Sources of Data: Department of Commerce, Office of Business Economics, Board of Governors of the Federal Reserve System.

1920's, the big boom until 1929, all finally culminating in the
Great Depression of the 1930's, which did not really come to
an end until the early days of World War II.

DEPRESSION

Twenty or even ten years ago it would not have been
necessary to ask, what does it mean in human terms to
undergo a depression of the magnitude of the nineteen-thirties.
However, many readers will not have had personal experiences
of that period, and it certainly helps to appreciate the New
Economics when it is realized just how deep the depths of
such a depression can be.

A few statistics will help to show the impact. For one,
between 1930–32 about 5,000 banks (nearly a quarter of all
those in existence) failed, meaning a whole or partial loss of
their accumulated savings by about nine million people. For
another, the average farmer earned about $1000 in 1929; that
was down to $288 in 1932 and the rate of foreclosures on

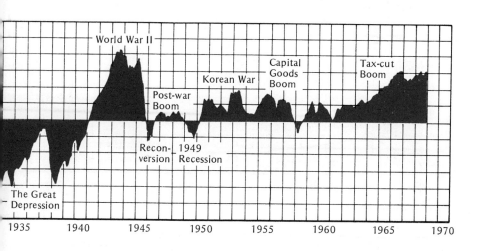

farm mortgages doubled. Meanwhile, business profits sank to zero and the failure rate for business went up by one-half, and construction activity fell to only 5% of its 1929 level.[9]

For workers the Great Depression was cataclysmic: for those who stayed employed the average weekly wage was down by about a third (in Chicago, working girls had wages of 10¢ per hour or less) but the problem was far worse for those who lost their jobs. Unemployment reached an official 13 million in 1933, or 25% of the labor force. Due to unprecedented difficulties in gathering statistics as people surged about the country looking for work, even this total may be a serious underestimate and some authorities put the figure at closer to 20 million unemployed. Consumer spending fell from nearly $40 billion to just over $20 billion, while personal saving out of income earned simply disappeared. This was bad enough in its own right, but the situation was made far worse by the impossibility of pulling up stakes and heading for the western frontier—the traditional safety valve for depressions of the nineteenth century.

Living conditions during the Great Depression were appalling, and must seem incredible to anyone who did not live through the 1930's. Formerly prosperous workers and businessmen could be seen on street corners selling apples,

Figure 1-2
Commodity Price Index

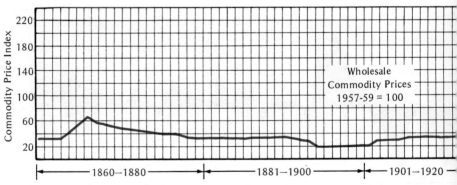

Source of Data: Department of Labor.

---

[9]For a compelling examination of the Great Depression, Arthur Schlesinger Jr., Crisis of the Old Order (Boston: Houghton-Mifflin Co., 1957) is hard to beat. Several of the examples noted above appear in that volume.

and at night they would go "home" to tarpaper shacks, or old car bodies, or discarded packing cases near the railroad yards or the town dump, which they, with no little venom, named "Hoovervilles." In the Bowery of New York 2,000 people were in the breadlines every day.

If only President Hoover had had the assistance of a dozen —or even only one or two—economists who understood the principles of the New Economics, then the immense human and money cost of the Great Depression might have been avoided.[10]

Unfortunately, at this period the New Economics was still a thing of the future. Consequently, the country suffered through a decade of unemployment which in money terms was equal to the cost of fighting a major war of World War II proportions.

INFLATION

In comparison to the misery of a full-scale slump, inflation seems much the lesser evil. However, the adverse impact of inflation, which may be defined as a general rise in the level of prices, should not be underestimated. Whenever this

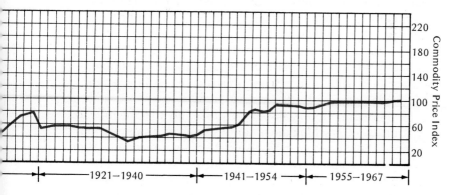

———|←———— 1921–1940 ————→|←——— 1941–1954 ——→|←—— 1955–1967 ——→|

---

[10]*The causes of the Great Depression still are debated in academic circles. But the medicine to effect a cure, which is examined in the central sections of this book, would almost certainly have enabled us to avoid most of the rigors of that disastrous decade.*

country has suffered through serious inflations—and it can
be seen in Figure 1–2 that the price level more than doubled
between 1860 and 1865, 1917 and 1920, and 1940 to 1950—
the adverse effects are readily perceived.

As prices rise *some* people are going to benefit: businessmen
for instance may establish their own selling prices by putting
a percentage markup on their costs of production. So as all
prices rise, the businessman will not fall behind nor will the
stockholders who share in the profits of corporations.

But there are losers too. Inflation changes the relative
income levels of the members of society, sometimes in a
radical fashion. Persons with fixed income find themselves
losing ground, for example those who depend upon insurance
payments, bond interest, and pensions, all usually fixed in
amount. Social Security payments may also be fixed for long
periods, and although this has been less true in 1968–1971,
rises in Social Security benefits almost always amount to
playing a game of "catch up" with inflation. Then too salary
earners may find it difficult to get their salaries adjusted
upward in time to keep up with steadily rising prices. Some
wage earners may be in the same boat, though where there
are strong labor unions workers may be able to keep pace
with the inflation.

The same phenomenon of falling behind affects wealth, as
accumulated savings lose in value. For instance, $1000 in the
bank in 1938 would buy you only something less than $400
worth of goods today, because of the intervening price
increases. Nor does the inflation have to proceed at a very fast
rate for this to happen. A little arithmetic will show that an
annual rate of price increase of 5%, about what we suffered
during 1970, will halve in the short space of just 14 years the
purchasing power of a dollar saved now.

Furthermore, there is always the possibility that the inflation
will run away, reaching the notorious stage of *hyper*inflation
when a whole nation can reach a state of semi-madness. Aside
from our Revolutionary War experience, and the Southern
Confederacy in the Civil War, we have fortunately not been
close to hyperinflation in this country, but elsewhere there
have been more recent cases of this violent disease. For
instance, in Germany during 1923 the postage stamps for one
ordinary letter cost billions of Deutsche Marks, far greater than
the total quantity of the whole German money supply in

existence just 10 years before; four trillion Marks were equal in value to about one American dollar; and a bank account in which a person might have been putting his savings for a lifetime, would, because of the inflation, not give enough to buy a pack of cigarettes. Interest rates were over 900%, and wages were sometimes adjusted several times a day.

And this is not the worst example. China had an equally bad hyperinflation when Chiang Kai–Shek was still on the mainland, but Hungary topped them all in 1946 when one US dollar equalled 30 quintillion Hungarian pengoes (that's 30 followed by 18 zeros). Fortunately, hyperinflations are always associated with wild printing of new money by the government, so that even a minimum of monetary prudence will avoid these consequences.[11]

The fact should still be remembered that even a mild inflation brings some serious consequences, particularly for the elderly and others on fixed incomes and that periodic bouts of inflation have been part and parcel of American historical experience.

Hopefully enough has been said by now on the topics of depression and inflation to carry the point that *both* have been with us since the beginning of our Republic, and that both afflictions, with the bag of troubles they bring, are among the great social problems to be faced by ours or any other government.

KEYNES AND THE NEW ECONOMICS

Nearly forty years ago, in 1936, a senior professor at Cambridge University in England published a book with a long and unimpressive title. The author was John Maynard Keynes,[12] the title was *The General Theory of Employment, Interest, and Money,* and the effect was an intellectual revolution which brought into being the New Economics.

11*The inveterate browser interested in this topic can find much pleasure in the annual editions of Stanley Gibbons' postage stamp catalogues, which picture the stamps of all countries. When hyperinflations are in progress it is sometimes necessary to leave blank spaces in the center of the stamps so that postmasters can write in the requisite large number of zeroes.*
12*Pronounced "Kanes" not "Kines."*

The decades of uncontrolled inflation and depression, and in particular the Great Depression of the 1930's, had at long last forced the profession of economics, as personified by Keynes, to reevaluate the threadbare classical theories.

We must not think of Keynes as a writer of lucid prose who was immediately to rescue the world from the cycles of boom and bust. Rather, his turgid book is replete with unfathomable technical jargon.[13] It is not an easy book, and yet it contained the basic principles for the operation of a modern economy which, when finally understood by governments in the 1960's, came to make up our arsenal of weapons against inflation and depression.

John Maynard Keynes (made Lord Keynes four years before his death in 1946) was a most interesting man. From his revolutionary ideas on the involvement of government in economic life, it might be thought that he was a radical, perhaps a man who would today belong to the New Left.[14]

The truth is quite the opposite; as noted earlier, he was a professor at Cambridge University, and he had no affinity with political radicalism (he *was* born in 1883, the year Karl Marx died.)

Like his countryman Adam Smith he traveled in high circles and was an acquaintance of Churchill and Roosevelt, Picasso, and George Bernard Shaw. Besides being an economist, he was a prominent mathematician, and more or less along the way had accumulated a personal fortune of about two million dollars from his hobby of staying in bed to read his morning paper, then placing a buy or sell order for an international currency or commodity.[15] Keynes was a bit eccentric; to this day his unorthodox social life and marriage to a prima ballerina

---

13As an example of his prose, the beginning of the critical theoretical passage which is the heart of the book runs "Let Z be the aggregate supply price of the output from employing N men, the relationship between Z and N being written $Z=f(N)$, which can be called the Aggregate Supply Function."

14An essay concerning him is included in chapter 9 of Heilbroner's Worldly Philosophers (op. cit.).

15Kenneth Boulding relates the story (for which he will not vouch) that Keynes once asked to borrow the magnificent and hallowed old Kings College chapel at Cambridge for a few days. "The chaplain was overjoyed at this evidence of conversion of a noted infidel until it turned out that Keynes had got caught short with a load of wheat in the course of his speculations in futures [prices] and wanted to use the chapel for storage." See Boulding's Economics as a Science (New York: McGraw-Hill, 1970), p. 133.

attract comment from his biographers. He first came to prominence at the close of World War I when he wrote a scathing and deserved attack on the Treaty of Versailles called *The Economic Consequences of the Peace.* From that time he had the position and the opportunity to contemplate the descending spiral in which the world found itself during the Great Depression.

SUMMARY

Given this brief history, our task in the remaining chapters of this book will be to delineate the ways in which Keynes and later proponents of the New Economics show how to combat inflation and depression. We will take care to discuss both the successes and failures of this policy.

Even though Keynes' *General Theory* is over thirty years old, the term New Economics is still highly appropriate, because unfortunately acceptance of Keynes' theories has been very slow. Today there remains widespread lack of knowledge among the general population as to the central principles of the New Economics, particularly concerning the government's responsibility for maintaining a stable economy. Certainly this lack of knowledge is shared by some US Congressmen, among whom opposition to the New Economics is still frequently encountered. Of the other advanced nations, only West Germany has been slower than the US to adopt Keynesian ideas.

Without some understanding of these ideas and their development it is not possible to follow some of the most important political debates of our time. It is thought, for instance, that the poor performance of the American economy in the years before 1960 and the recriminations as to what policy should have been followed contributed heavily to President Kennedy's victory and to Mr. Nixon's defeat. Whereas in 1964 prosperity helped the Democratic "ins," in 1968 poor use of the New Economics—the fault lying not entirely with one party but with both —provided powerful ammunition for the Republican "outs." 1972 promises much more of the same, with general agreement that the state of the economy stands as the paramount issue of the campaign.

We need only to open our daily newspapers to find the

political content of these arguments confirmed as we read that President Nixon is being hurt by the current high levels of inflation and unemployment, or that over-reaction by the government may plunge the economy into a depression. The headlines of Monday morning, August 15, 1971, announcing the boldest, most unexpected economic reform in 40 years, and which tacitly admitted the failure of the old Nixon "stand-pat" game plan of economic strategy, can be understood very imperfectly without some acquaintance with the rules of modern economic management. In short, intelligent opinion and reasoned political decision-making call for, at the very least, a minimal familiarity with the New Economics.[16]

---

[16]*Economists use the term "macroeconomics" to describe the area covered by the Keynesian theories. In this volume, the phase "New Economics" is used as a less forbidding synonym.*

Questions

1. What was the failure of the "Old Economics"?
2. What evidence would you advance in debating the proposition "The US economy has been remarkably stable since this country's independence?"
3. What are the social consequences of depression? Of inflation?

2.

MEASURING ECONOMIC PERFORMANCE

In the last chapter, we established that inflation and depression recurred regularly in the history of capitalism in the US, and that both have extremely serious social consequences. The former brings unemployment and reduced output; the latter eats away at the value of fixed incomes such as pensions, at savings, and at other forms of accumulated wealth.

As we have mentioned, the Keynesian or New Economics proposes modern ways of analyzing inflation and depression, and suggests methods in which these old afflictions can be controlled or even eliminated by the preventive medicine of economic policy.

Thus we turn to our main topic: what *is* this new method of analysis and how can it be used as a basis for policy decisions? One fact should be self-evident: it would be very difficult, perhaps impossible, to depict with accuracy an economy's performance without first acquiring for it a reasonable system of measurement.

NATIONAL PRODUCT

For purposes of policy action, governments must move to attack inflation or depression long before they become serious;

both are much harder to defeat after they become entrenched. That is one reason why the present method of evaluating the economy's performance is so important to understand, for like a network of early warning radar, it allows economic counteraction to be taken early instead of too late. Readers who have no acquaintance with the various measuring rods will be at a big disadvantage in understanding why governments change economic policies as they do.

The system of measurement currently in use is very modern indeed, and it may come as a surprise to learn that most of it is only about 30 years old—the child of the Great Depression and World War II.

During the 1930's, rapid growth of unemployment and cuts in wages meant a sharp decline in the amount of income earned by the general public. The government found that this drop in income tended to upset the federal budget, because tax collections fell accordingly.[1] There were thus the alternatives of cutting back government spending to the level of reduced tax collections, of raising the rates of taxation, or of borrowing. It is easy to appreciate the government's desire to consider these alternatives well in advance, and understand how this led to the development of a method of measurement.

At the same time, economists had come to realize that government spending and tax policies had a significant impact on the total figure for spending in the economy. This also led to the search for some quantifiable way to gauge that impact.

World War II was of great importance in the development of a system of measurement, because both in the US and abroad governments had to assess rapidly how much total output was possible. This led to overall surveys of available resources, particularly labor and raw materials. The US government knew that production could not exceed that which could be obtained when all resources were fully employed; that therefore output targets if placed above this level would not be attained, resulting in shortages and bottlenecks; and finally that *less* output than the maximum obtainable with all resources employed would be inefficient and would lessen the war effort. Thus programs were instituted to determine what portion of the country's output was produced in the different sectors of American industry.

---

[1] *As will be more fully explained later, when taxes are based primarily upon incomes, and incomes fall, then tax receipts must decline.*

Meanwhile it was necessary to estimate how much output had to be devoted to civilian consumption in the form of food, clothing, housing, transportation, etc., to keep the nonmilitary part of the population at some minimal standard of living. These were the main reasons why a method of economic accounting was developed.

So much for historical antecedents. The salient fact is that the New Economics could have made little progress without a reasonably accurate measure of what was going on in the economy—a measure that was simply not available until the middle 1930's at the earliest. It was developed during World War II, and is still being improved upon at present.

*   *   *

How is the TOTAL OUTPUT of a country measured?

This is done through the national income and national product accounts, which are examined here in sufficient detail for future use of these concepts.

The first and most common measure of total output is national product. This represents the nation's yearly production of goods and services. *Goods* are tangible items, such as autos, food, and clothing. *Services* are intangible items, like haircuts, the work of an insurance agent, the transport of goods by steamship, railway, or trucking company, a stay in a motel, a visit to the dentist.

There is only one way in which all these diverse items can be brought together—via dollar values which give a reasonable common denominator. The dollar value of a good or service produced during a given year is its market price, that is whatever is paid for it.

Thus in its most simple form, national product is the money value at market prices of the total national output of goods and services for one year.

It is customary and convenient (and will be significant later in the book) to break this measure down into several component parts. The sum total of the market value of goods and services produced in a given year (allowing a repeat of our definition of national product) can be divided into three sectors.

Some of this production is for consumers, called con-sumption or C. Some is investment (I). The latter is defined as the creation of man-made goods, called capital, which are designed to increase future output. Examples of investment might include construction of a factory building, a machine or a new railroad. Finally, some output is for the government, labelled G. This might include the services of the post office, a warship, or a new school.

Foreign trade also has a place in the national product, but as it is far less important in dollar terms than C, I, or G, and as its treatment is a bit complicated, it is omitted here.[2]

MEASUREMENT: DOUBLE COUNTING

When estimating the national product we must be very careful to avoid certain ticklish problems. The first and perhaps the greatest sin is called *double counting.* If you are valuing US production for 1972, for instance, what if you were to include all the wood pulp produced, all the paper produced, and all the books and newspapers produced? Do you see that you have included the value of the wood three times? This is because the value of the wood is naturally part of the value of the paper and of the book too.

The solution is to count only the item which *includes* the value of all intermediate goods; that is, count only the *final product* which in this case is the book or newspaper. Take an example: say a book costs $7. It would be a mistake to say national product should include 25¢ for the wood pulp, $1.00 for the paper, $5.75 for the book when sold at the publisher's warehouse, and finally $7.00 for the book when sold by the local retail bookseller, giving 25¢ + $1.00 + $5.75 + $7.00 = $14 in all. Because the wood, the paper, and the price of the book at the publisher are *all included* in the final price of the book at the bookstore.

This logic also extends to used or traded items. Any second-hand goods already sold once cannot be valued in the national product accounts because if something has already been sold, then it has at some former time, either this year or in some past year, been included. To do so again would be double counting. Nor should transfers be counted. Gifts when exchanged do not represent new production but simply a new owner. What if the present is a new good, however? In this case, it will have *already* been included in the national

---

[2]*Foreign trade will be considered in the last section of the book.*

accounts when produced and sold, and must not be included again when transferred from one person to another.

MEASUREMENT: INVESTMENT

There is a second problem with national product, more minor but one which will crop up again and with which the reader will want to be familiar. This has to do with investment. Some investment is for new capital, defined as new plant and equipment. Some other investment, new and shiny though it may be, is however meant as replacement for the old capital (plant and equipment) that has worn out and been retired from service. The two types taken together are called GROSS investment; when only additions to capital are counted, *not* including replacement, this is termed NET investment. Remember, though, sale and transfer of plant and equipment if it does not represent new production would be double counting and thus should not be included in this year's national product accounts.

MEASUREMENT: GOVERNMENT OUTPUT

A third and final problem has to do with the government. It is logical and correct to assume that some of the government's output will be destined for consumers and some will be for investment purposes. It may seem strange that no division is made here as was done with consumption (C) and investment (I) in the private sector of the economy. But by convention this is not done and government output, whether for consumption purposes or investment goods, is lumped together under the term G. As before, the sale of second-hand government goods must be excluded.

National product may thus be written $C + I + G$.

FACTORS OF PRODUCTION

In addition to the value of total output $(C + I + G)$ there is another way to look at national product. It is possible to ask, what is the TOTAL INCOME earned by the production of one year's goods and services? We may suspect that several kinds of income are likely to be earned in the production of any particular item, and economists speak generally of four elements that go into the production of an item, and thus stand to earn the incomes which accrue as a good is produced. These four, the so-called "factors of production," are broad categories which give a quick way to describe the inputs of an economy.

The first of the factors of production is LAND. Not just usable, arable land either, for the term is defined to include other aspects of land such as natural resources.

The second factor is LABOR. Here again more than the sheer volume of workers available in the production process is meant. Included also are such very important aspects as skill and education, which play a significant role in determining the quality of the labor force.

CAPITAL is the third factor. You will recall that capital was defined earlier, but perhaps it will be helpful to repeat: a short definition might be anything man-made which helps to increase production. Machines, tools, and buildings, for instance. One difference between this and the other factors of production which is easy to spot is that capital must be an input, a factor which at some stage has *already been* an output.

Last on the list is a fairly long-winded economic term, ENTREPRENEURSHIP or entrepreneurial ability. The term is related to the French word for enterprise, and that describes very well what is meant by this factor of production. The entrepreneur has three functions, all of which are vital in the production process. Firstly, he can be described as an initiator or innovator—he gets things going. Secondly, he is an organizer, whose aim is efficiency in production. Finally the entrepreneur is the risk–taker, risking funds, reputation, or both, in some project, and standing to lose or gain depending on the failure or success of his ideas. These, then, are the factors of production.

NATIONAL INCOME

Now back to the original point, that there is another way to measure the nation's output. What is the amount of income earned by each of the factors of production during one year's output of goods and services? Each of these factors will receive a different type of monetary reward. For labor, it is wages and salaries; for land, rent; for capital, interest (which is a complicated question in itself and will here simply be called the return to capital); and finally the profit that accrues to the entrepreneur when goods are sold. If we add these all together, wages and salaries + rent + interest + profit, we have the national income.

Analytically, this national income is going to be exactly the same as national product, and it is crucial to appreciate this definitional equality between a nation's income and its output. Take a very brief example which includes just one product like a color TV. Its money value was clearly counted as part of the national product if it was produced this year. Say its market price, counted in national product, is $300 and that is what it was sold for. Then people somewhere must have earned $300 in new income. Say the expense of producing the TV is $150 for labor, $25 for the natural resources used (land) and $100 for the expenses of using machines and other capital. COSTS thus total $275. The item was SOLD for $300. There is thus a profit of $25 left over. If profit, defined as whatever is left over after costs are paid out, is treated as somebody's income, (which it certainly is) then the INCOME EARNED from the sale of an item is identical to the market price at which the item is sold. When this example is repeated for all goods and services produced in an economy, then it becomes clear that the value of all output in a year is exactly equal to the income generated by this production. This is a point to which we shall return again and again in this book.

However, if the national income results from the production of output as described above, we must be careful *not* to include cash flows which do not stem from actual production. One such item is transfer payments. Government transfers including, for example, relief payments, veterans benefits, and social security outlays, are all praiseworthy and necessary no doubt, but they do *not* represent current production of any goods or services and thus ought not to be valued in the national product.

Private transfers must also be kept out of the national accounts. If Peter gives Paul a Christmas gift of cash, a real transfer of purchasing power has taken place all right, but the gift does not represent current income or output. Take another example: a share of common stock in a corporation. If this is sold by Pierpont to Morgan, a transfer takes place to be sure— Morgan gets the stock and Pierpont gets his money. But there is no current production nor income earned and the transaction is not valued in the national accounts, with the exception that if they do business through a stockbroker who makes his living by facilitating such transactions, this would be classed as a service and the broker's earnings would be put in the national income. However, the accounts do NOT include the whole price of the share but only the broker's commission, for that represents the value of his services. The same logic will apply to bonds, the sale of land, etc.

Questions

1. Why is it crucial for modern economic policy to have a system of measurement?
2. What is total output? Total income?
3. Why are total output and total income identical?
4. What are the factors of production?

3.

THE PROCESS
OF MEASUREMENT
AND
ITS FLAWS

The concept of national product and national income should now be reasonably clear, but in actual practice there are certain further questions that we ought to consider. The measurement of these values in actual practice involves some complexities which even a well-educated person might never suspect. If the reader ponders for a moment, he might even assume that since in all likelihood no government accountant has ever asked him how much *he* produces, then the official statistics are missing something.

In actual fact, totals for neither national product nor national income are obtained by a process of just adding up the values of goods produced or sold, or by compiling and adding together all incomes earned. As Richard and Nancy Ruggles write, "No single set of comprehensive reports specifically designed for national income and   product accounting purposes is available from which such compilations could be made. Instead, there are large masses of information from a wide variety of different sources that yield useful data on specific parts of the economy or on certain kinds of transactions, and these different sources must be integrated into the national accounting framework by building up the estimates piece by piece."[1]

What are the important pieces used for estimation? On the side of national income, perhaps the most widely used and comprehensive source of information is government tax data. This would include income taxes, the corporate tax, and social security taxes. Large chunks of wages and salaries, rent, interest, and profit can receive quite accurate coverage via this tax data. Supplemental data from agricultural censuses, sample surveys, etc., help to fill any gaps.

Far different methods are used in estimating the national product. There are periodic censuses of industry which give reasonable estimates of the output of goods. Services are much more difficult to handle; there are private surveys by trade groups, a census of business, surveys of education, sampling data, and various other bits of information to draw on.

Sometimes data is available which gives an accurate estimate for, say, 1967, because of a business census taken in that year. If the census is not repeated until 1970, and will not be repeated again until 1973, then to find the national product in the intervening years 1971 and 1972, it may be necessary to make estimates on the basis of the two so-called "benchmark years." This means finding the amount of increase (or decrease) in output between the two years 1967 and 1970, then applying that rate as an estimate for the national product of 1971 and 1972. This is always supplemented where possible, of course, by whatever additional data is available, thus providing a check on accuracy.

With all these different ways of arriving at statements of product and income, how reliable are the figures? Naturally no one can guarantee 100% reliability, but there is one test that seems eminently reasonable. It has just been shown that product and income, which in concept should be identical, are actually MEASURED using very different sources of information. (As when we noted above the predominance of tax data in estimating income and census of business data in estimating product.) Thus, a LARGE discrepancy between national income and product would show that at least one of

---

[1]National Income Accounts and Income Analysis (New York: McGraw-Hill, 2nd edition, 1956), p. 158.

the estimates was erroneous, whereas a small discrepancy between the two should indicate a reasonably high degree of accuracy. Fortunately in actual experience it is almost uniformly true in the US that the margin of error between national product and national income has been quite small.[2]

GROSS AND NET NATIONAL PRODUCT

Since the concept of national product and income has been explained it is important to note a few variations which any literate person ought to understand if he is to keep up with what appears in the newspapers, and if he is to make rational decisions on economic issues.

The most common figure is GROSS national product, or GNP. We recall from the last chapter that we have already used the word GROSS. *Part* of national product is investment: C + I + G = national product. Remember that investment can be considered gross (including replacement of worn-out machines, etc.) or net (not including replacement but only *net additions* to the stock of capital). Thus GROSS national product *includes* gross investment. During 1971 it was expected that US GNP would be a little over one trillion dollars.

Another measure, NET national product or NNP is the same as GNP except that it includes only net investment and not the replacement of worn-out capital goods. Thus to the extent that capital goods do wear out, or *depreciate*, GNP differs from NNP and GNP minus depreciation (often called capital consumption) = NNP. The annual figure for depreciation, and hence the difference between gross and net national product, is usually a little less than 10% of GNP.

We have noted that the national income conceptually is the same as national product since the *price* of a good will represent the income earned by the factors of production

---

[2]*Department of Commerce estimates show the so-called "statistical discrepancy" to be about 1/4 of 1% in 1968, 1/2 of 1% in 1969, and 1/5 of 1% in 1970. The last period of really large gaps between income and product was during World War II when black markets were operating to evade government price controls.*

involved in its creation: wages and salaries for labor, rent for land including natural resources, interest as the return on capital, and whatever is left over going as profit to the entrepreneur or group of entrepreneurs who have provided the initiative and organization for a project and are assuming the risk of success or failure.

But for one important reason the measured figure for national income is going to be slightly *less* than the figure for net national product. The reason for this is that businessmen must pay certain taxes (called "indirect business taxes") before they become income to anyone. These include excise and sales taxes. For example an item sells for $1.00 without tax. With a 5% sales tax a businessman is going to collect $1.05 when the good changes hands. The 5 cents must be paid directly to the government, but it is not anyone's income nor is it income to the government either because it did nothing productive in the way of furnishing land, labor, capital, or entreprenurial ability for the manufacture of the good. The 5 cents IS part of the national product, however, as it is part of the market price at which the good was sold. But as it does not represent income, it cannot be counted in the figure for national income.

Thus GNP minus depreciation minus indirect business taxes equals the national income. US national income was about $810 billion in early 1971.

PROFIT

We have already noted that the national income is made up of wages and salaries, rent, interest, and profit. If, however, you look up these figures in the official government statistical bulletins or check on them in an economics textbook, you will run into something of a problem—profit. Corporations commonly employ accountants to determine exactly what their profits are in a given year.

But what about the owner of the corner grocery store or small laundry—men who are self-employed? Tradesmen of this type, running "single proprietorships" as owner-operated business are often called, will commonly keep books showing that after all costs of the business are met, whatever income is left over belongs to them and is called by them, their profits.

The problem is that part of these so-called profits actually represent NOT a return to the businessman's entrepreneurial function (initiating, organizing, taking risks) but is instead a return for his work as clerk, cashier, butcher, etc. Logically, then, part of the profits reported by individual proprietors should fall in the category of wages.

The government takes account of this in a simple way. It does not even attempt to solve the puzzle of what should go where, but just inserts another category along with wages and salaries, rent, interest, and profit, called proprietor's income. Part of this is actually wages, as we have noted, and part is profit. Naturally, the official figure for wages and salaries is lower than it would be otherwise, and the official figure for profit is only that part of profit which can be accurately ascertained; namely, *corporate* profit.

PERSONAL INCOME

However, of the total income earned in an economy, some is never actually received by the individuals who make up the general public. Take the corporate profits we were discussing a moment ago. *Some* of this profit is clearly shared by the general public via dividends. When corporations pay dividends, as that name implies, they are "dividing" their profits among their stockholders. But other portions of corporate profit would not be expected to follow this route. For instance, what about the income taxes eventually paid by corporations? And what about the earnings that companies keep to plow back into the business, called "undistributed corporate profits." The individuals who make up the general public will not share these two portions of the economic pie.

Other examples include social security taxes, deducted from your paycheck before you ever cash it. Your *earned* income must be reduced by that amount if we are to discover how much usable income you are going to be left with. And finally, there are various personal taxes which must be paid and are not available for your own use—the federal income tax being by far the most important.

Thus from national income we may SUBTRACT corporate taxes, undistributed corporate profit, social security taxes, and personal taxes to find what is actually retained. Oftentimes, on the other hand, some of the money available to an individual does not represent earned income but is nonetheless at his disposal. Examples of this include such items as social security payments, other welfare and pension funds and payments, relief, veteran's benefits, and any other government transfer payments.

When these are added to national income, and undistributed corporate profits, corporate taxes, social security taxes, and personal taxes are subtracted, the result is a figure which is defined to reflect, more accurately than does national income, the amount available for actual spending or saving by the general public. This figure is called, reasonably enough, DISPOSABLE PERSONAL INCOME.

The main problem with disposable personal income is that it is made public only every three months. The figure is much easier to estimate if the attempt is not made to subtract personal taxes, such as the income tax, because such taxes are hard to estimate with a high degree of accuracy over a shorter period than three months. When personal taxes are not subtracted, the resulting figure is called PERSONAL INCOME, as distinct from DISPOSABLE personal income, and measures of personal income are actually made available more frequently than are any others: nowadays on a once-a-month schedule. The monthly announcements of personal income often receive wide publicity, as during the present inflation-cum-unemployment, when they give an early indication of trends in the economy.

Our discussion can be summarized as follows:[3]

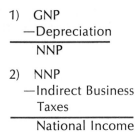

1) GNP
    —Depreciation
    ————————
    NNP

2) NNP
    —Indirect Business
    Taxes
    ————————
    National Income

---

[3]A few minor items are omitted in this enumeration. See any good principles of economics textbook for details.

3) National Income
    —Corporate taxes
    —Undistributed
    Corporate Profit
    —Social Security Taxes
    +Government Transfer
    Payments
    _____
    Personal Income

4) Personal Income
    —Personal Taxes
    _____
    Disposable Personal Income

GNP: NOT A PERFECT MEASURING ROD

For all our dependence on national income and national product accounts, and as indispensable as they are in developing the Keynesian principles of the New Economics, they have certain defects which must be kept in mind. Failure to do so may give an incorrect picture of an economy, or possibly lead to bad planning or bad policy.

Examples abound where unquestioning use of the national accounts have led someone astray. Consider such statements as, "US GNP has doubled in recent years, thus we are twice as well off as we were." Or, "China's GNP is larger than India's, so China's population is possessed of a higher standard of welfare and well-being."

These uses of GNP as an indicator of welfare, or standard of living, either over time or between different countries, involve some serious problems, and even the absolute level of GNP in a given year involves some arbitrary decisions as to how it should be measured.

One easy and obvious point must spring to mind very quickly. If an economist tries to estimate the level of welfare or well-being of a nation, over time or in comparison with another country, he must clearly take into account any change in the size of the population (or difference in the number of people if he compares countries). It would be senseless to compare US and British standards of living by looking at their total GNP because the US has more people. The only accurate solution is to take a figure for product, or income,

PER CAPITA, meaning per person. This is done via the simple arithmetical maneuver of dividing the total product or income figure by the size of the population. For the US, our 800 billion dollar national income makes Britain's 100-odd billion (when converted into dollars) look puny, but when it is remembered that the US has 200 million people and Britain only a little over 50 million, we see that the PER CAPITA incomes are much closer: 800 billion dollars divided by 200 million people in the US gives about $4,000 per person; greater but not overwhelmingly so than Britain's $100 million divided by 50 million which equals about $2,000 per person.

There are some further difficulties. Accuracy will be affected by the fact that certain production is most definitely output but never gets sold on the market. Take the services of a housewife–cooking, cleaning, taking care of children. This *would* be valued in the GNP if it were done by a maid or waitress as a service, but it is felt that the difficulties and ambiguities of measurement are sufficiently great that the government simply excludes housewives' services from the GNP. Someone will be tempted to say his wife just nags and watches TV all day anyway, so we're not missing any output by not counting her, but in all seriousness it is thought that several hundred billion dollars worth of output which in concept should be valued is omitted.

There are some similar exclusions which represent output that is very difficult to estimate because it is not sold on the market. A familiar example is do-it-yourself work in the home (carpentry, housepainting, plumbing) etc.

To continue briefly with some further problems, comparisons of any kind which attempt to equate GNP or income with welfare or the standard of living bring difficulties of the following type:

LEISURE. Since the 1920's in the US, the work week has declined to about 60% of its old level. Leisure is highly regarded by practically everyone, but as it is not output, it is not included in national income or product at all.

Then there is the term used by economists, PSYCHIC INCOME. This means that some output carries with it psychological or "inner" satisfaction—work as a nurse, doctor, teacher, for example—which may be entirely unreflected in the national accounting. Conversely, other output—a rendering works, a glue factory, garbage disposal, repetitious assembly-line work—all these may bring *dis*satisfaction to whoever is employed in these occupations which is similarly ignored in the national accounting, where as usual, output and income are included only in dollar values and without considering any underlying psychic reaction.

There is the additional problem of WHAT GOODS are produced. War goods? Investment goods (machines, factories, etc.) as traditionally in the Soviet Union? Consumer goods? Products which carry with them social costs such as polluted streams and air? The product mix chosen will certainly affect standards of well-being, but this will not show up in the totals of the national account.

Then, DISTRIBUTION. It is obvious that there is a difference in satisfaction or welfare depending on who *gets* the goods. An observer would expect a far different climate of opinion in a country with a few very rich citizens and many who are very poor, in comparison with a country where the distribution of income, that is the sharing in the goods and services produced, is more or less equal.

QUALITY is another point. GNP does not reflect improvements in the quality of a product, except insofar as its price changes. Per dollar spent, many items from electric light bulbs to cars have better performance and more reliability than they did 30 years ago. Some goods may perform less well. Either way, these factors are not included in the GNP although they may very much influence the standard of living.

Lastly, and of great importance, PRICE CHANGES make year-to-year comparisons more difficult. GNP might be $450 billion this year and $900 billion next year, and we might all be very pleased at this. But what if prices of all items, on average, have doubled in the meantime? Then the real change in output has been zero and the doubling in GNP has been illusory, caused only by the price rise.

We can allow for this via a PRICE INDEX. If all prices have doubled our price index will be 200%, or 2. We divide the GNP figure by the price index, in this case $\dfrac{\$900\ \text{billion},}{2}$

to get the so-called REAL GNP, i.e., that GNP which is based on the price level in some previous year. That is why in newspapers you will often run across figures such as "1971

GNP based on 1958 prices"—the writer is simply trying to cancel the effect of changes in the general price level over time.

We have now completed our study of national income and product, and should have a sufficient economic background at this point so that in the next chapter the unravelling of the Keynesian principles of the New Economics can begin.

Questions

1. What are some of the methods used by the US government to measure national product? National income?
2. What do the words gross, net, capital consumption and depreciation, have to do with national product?
3. Why are there several different measures of income, and what are they?
4. What are the criticisms which can be made of the national accounts as a measure of welfare and standard of living?

4.

CONSUMPTION INVESTMENT SAVING: Keystones in the Keynesian Framework

The last two chapters showed how the idea of national product and national income were conceived, and how they are measured. This chapter will consider two simple lessons from that discussion.

You will recall that national product can be divided into three categories. The first of these is output of consumption goods, labeled C. Second is investment (I), and lastly there is government (G). And as already shown, $C + I + G =$ the National Product.

It is also possible to divide the national INCOME into categories, and this too was done in the past two chapters when income was seen to include wages and salaries, rent, interest and profit.

Now for the introduction of a new idea. The national income can also be discussed in terms of its disposal. In other words, once income is earned, what do people do with it? There are actually three general ways in which income is used. People can spend their earnings for consumption, including the consumption of both goods and services which we can again label C. They can save (indicated by S). Finally, they can, or rather they MUST pay taxes, which we may label Gt. Since by definition the general public acts in these three ways with the income it earns, then $C + S + Gt =$ the National Income.

For the time being, the government sector will be omitted for the sake of simplicity. Again, simplicity is also the reason for not considering the exports and imports which make up foreign trade.[1]

If this is the case, National Product $(C + I + G)$ becomes just $C + I$, as we can now leave off the G, while on the side of National Income $(C + S + Gt)$, we can ignore government taxes, leaving only $C + S$. Thus for now $C + S$ will represent the uses to which the national income may be put.

The next chapter will show that the relationship between $C + I$ and $C + S$ is really the heart of the New Economics. The case will be made that $C + I$ and $C + S$, with government temporarily omitted, are crucial in determining whether national income will rise or fall; whether a country is bedeviled by inflation, or caught in a slump with workers going unemployed and depression taking hold.

But first we must try to discover what it is that DETERMINES consumption, saving, and investment, so that in chapter 5 when we begin to unravel the importance of the relationship between them, we will already have some knowledge of how their levels have been established.

CONSUMPTION

By far the most important in money terms of any of the three ingredients in our Keynesian stew is consumption. In any year —and not just any normal year, for what follows has applied in war years and times of depression as well—the level of consumption is much greater than that of saving, or investment, or government spending. Recently about 80% of all income earned has been spent for personal consumption— after taxes. If we abide by our earlier assumption and keep

---

[1]Omitting the government sector does not change the analysis in any critical way, as will be seen in chapter 7, although changing the level of government activity is crucial to modern economic management. Omitting government also has a reasonable historical precedent, because when Keynes wrote in 1936, and through all the earlier decades in both the United States and in foreign countries, government spending and taxation as a percentage of national product and income were very much smaller than they have been since Keynes.

Concerning foreign trade, recall again that imports and exports appear in more advanced works but are not treated here. Both can be fitted into the framework with no great difficulty, however.

government out of the picture, then on an average this country has utilized over 90% of its income for consumption purposes, and less than 10% for saving.

One fact should be fairly clear. Barring the government, anything which determines the level of consumption will automatically be a determinant of the level of saving. This must be true if whatever is not spent for consumption is therefore saved, which is the case as long as we do not have to worry about taxation.

An important element in the New Economics is understanding that the *most significant* determining factor in the level of consumption is the level of income that people have to spend.[2] There is even a measure which is most useful here. The last chapter showed a variation in measuring national income which reflects with more accuracy the amount of money people actually had available for spending—disposable personal income. This figure, "disposable income," gives an excellent indication of what consumption will be in any period of time. And do not forget, a figure for consumption is also a figure for saving, since in the simple C + S theory what is not consumed is saved. The accompanying chart helps to illustrate this relationship. Presume that the nation's disposable income can vary over a range from low to high, perhaps from $400 billion up to a figure of $700 billion. Given that income could be anywhere within this range, (column one of Table 4–1 shows seven possibilities) then economists can try to estimate what people would want to or plan to consume at these various income levels.

TABLE 4–1

(1)	(2)	(3)
DISPOSABLE INCOME ($ billion)	PLANNED CONSUMPTION ($ billion)	PLANNED SAVING ($ billion)
400	410	−10
450	450	0
500	490	10
550	530	20
600	570	30
650	610	40
700	650	50

2Though economists do debate whether present income, past income or expected future income is most important.

Why the emphasis on what people "want to" or "plan to" consume at this income level? The reason for this is not difficult, but important. Something might happen in the meantime (and we will be trying to discover what that something is) to *change* the level of national income, so that when the time actually arrives for spending there is either more or less income on hand than was initially expected. Thus consumption will have to be higher or lower than originally planned. So, to make things easier, we say only that assuming one of these levels of national income, what will people *want to consume?*

The figures in the second column show possible levels of what people would want to consume at various given incomes. As is to be expected, where the level of income is very low the planned level of consumption is also low. So low in the case of the second figure, $450 billion, that people feel too poor to want to save anything, and even worse at $400 billion where people are actually consuming more than they earn in income, living off their savings at the rate of $10 billion per year. Conversely, at high incomes people want to increase their consumption a great deal, as is shown by the figures toward the bottom of the table.

SAVING

What about saving? Remember, that which is not consumed is saved, leading to the third column in the chart. Recall that where income is $450 billion, people want to consume $450 billion worth of goods and services, and planned saving is zero. At $500 billion income, desired consumption is $490 billion and planned saving $10 billion. At the high level of income $700 billion, the difference between income and consumption gives us the much greater figure for savings of $50 billion.

All this can be pictured on diagrams which can be used to illustrate the relationship between income and consumption. Figure 4–2 is a graph with two axes, of the type practically everyone will have met with at one time or another in a high school mathematics class. On the horizontal axis[3] is measured the level of income, starting at zero at the far left and running past the break which will allow the chart to be kept within reasonable bounds, up to the figure of $700 billion.[4]

On the vertical axis[5] is planned consumption, again running from zero, past a break to keep the size in bounds, up to $600 billion.

Note that if income should happen to be at a level of $450 billion, the figures in our earlier Table (4–1) confirm that the public wants to consume also to the tune of $450 billion. We

FIGURE 4-2

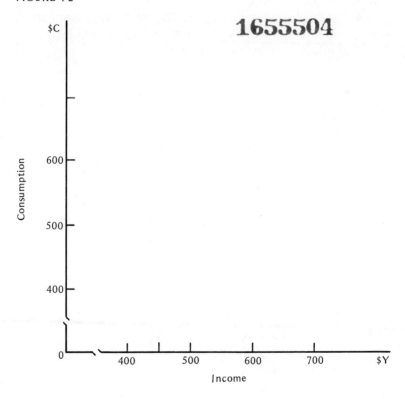

could make a point on a graph and mark it A (on Figure 4–3);
see how this position indicates an income of $450 billion and
planned consumption of $450 billion. And what IF for example,
at income $400 billion people wanted to consume $400
billion? The point showing this would be at B. Similarly,
income $600 billion and planned consumption $600 billion
would give a point C.

From all this a rule becomes evident. Whenever people plan
to use for consumption all the income that they earn, as in
the examples above, points appear on the graph which are
equidistant from each axis. And if these points are connected
by a line, then that line forms a 45° angle at the base, giving
it its name: the 45° line.

A 45° line, when drawn in on the diagram, is very useful in
that it can show us ALL POINTS where income would be
destined totally for use as consumption.

FIGURE 4-3

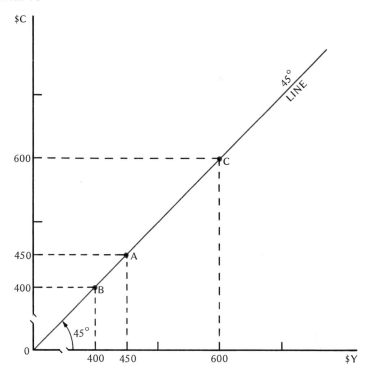

CONSUMPTION SCHEDULE

Now the information already contained in our earlier Table 4-1 and already discussed, can be pictured graphically (Figure 4-4) showing the hypothetical data as to what the public would want to consume at any level of disposable income.

Take $400 billion of income. Consumption planned is $410 billion. At $450 billion intended consumption is $450 billion. At $500 billion planned consumption is $490 billion—all the way up to an income of $700 billion where the public wishes to consume $650 billion. In all this, note that from the point which shows the income along the horizontal axis, the vertical distance up to the line drawn to connect the points measures the level of planned consumption. Economists call this line the CONSUMPTION SCHEDULE. (C).

FIGURE 4-4

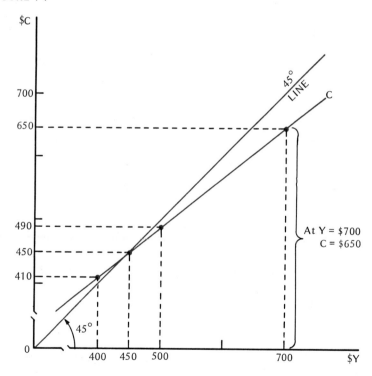

What about saving on the graph? Where does this appear, if it does at all?

Here is the prime reason why that 45° line was drawn in. As pointed out earlier, whatever income is not consumed is saved. Remember that the distance from the horizontal axis to the consumption schedule represents planned consumption. Remember also that if we go all the way up to the 45° line at any level of income, then by our rule all income that is earned will be used for consumption. The *difference* between the two lines, that is the vertical distance between them, must represent that portion of income not consumed, thus, saved. Try an example (Figure 4–5): at an income level of $600 billion, our consumption schedule tells us that the public wants to consume $570 billion. The distance between the two lines must be whatever is left over, and amounts to $30 billion. (Which is what the table of figures told us to expect in the first place.)

FIGURE 4-5

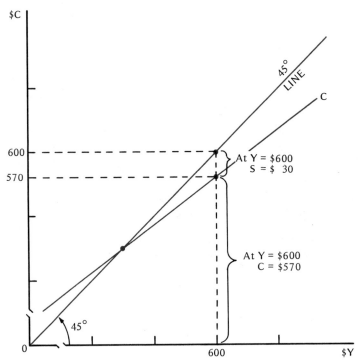

Notice that in all of this nothing has been said about the rate of interest and what that has to do with determining how much is saved. After all, it would seem reasonable to suppose that you will save far more, by putting cash into a savings account for instance, when the interest rate is 5% as compared to when your money will earn only, say, 3% for you. But early in the Keynesian Revolution, when the New Economics was being developed, economists discovered the surprising fact that the interest rate is very, very much less important than the size of a person's income in determining what he wants to save. This point will become very significant in a later chapter.

CONSUMPTION SCHEDULE: NON-INCOME DETERMINANTS

Although we have been at pains to show that income is the major determinant of consumption and saving, there are certain so-called "non-income" determinants which do from time to time exert their own influence on consumption and saving. Five important ones are noted below.

First, future expectations as to prices and incomes help to determine consumption. Assume people believe that prices will rise sharply in the near future; or that their incomes are due to increase. In both cases the tendency may be to buy now rather than later. And if the story is reversed, giving an expectation of falling prices in the future, or of reduced incomes, this will influence the spender to put off some consumption.

Second is the general view of thriftiness. Is it that of Benjamin Franklin, with his "He that goes a borrowing goes a sorrowing," "Remember that time is money," "A penny saved is a penny earned." Or is the nation caught up with Thorstein Veblen's Conspicuous Consumption, where we consume ever greater amounts as an exercise in ostentation to "Keep up with the Joneses."[6]

Third is stocks of durable goods—goods like cars and refrigerators that tend to last for several years. Consumption of these will be promoted after, say, a war when many durables

---

[6]Veblen, one of the most interesting personalities ever to grace the economics profession (if "grace" can be used for a man with his idiosyncrasies), is discussed at length in Heilbroner's Worldly Philosophers.

have worn out and need replacement, whereas after a period
of prosperity there may be a surfeit of durables, lessening
consumption on that account.

Fourth are the holdings by the general public of stocks,
bonds, insurance policies, bank accounts, etc.—liquid assets as
they are termed by economists. The greater these holdings
the richer a person will ordinarily feel and the more he will
be tempted to use for consumption out of a given level of
income as opposed to saving.

Fifth and last is the level of debt. The more saddled people
are with debts, the less likely they are to spend. (Though the
rising numbers of personal bankruptcies show that this is not
necessarily a correct assumption for everybody.)

Here is something to keep firmly in mind. Whenever any
one of the circumstances just discussed is altered—say a lower
level of private debt, or greater propensity to keep up with the
Joneses—what this means is that at ANY level of income on
our charts, the desire to consume and save has changed. Take
the consumption schedule. If people decide to be more
thrifty, then notwithstanding whether income is relatively low
—as at A in Figure 4–6, middling as at B, or high as at C, the
whole consumption schedule will shift downward all along
its length to C_1. The point is that whatever the income, people
just do not desire to consume as much as they had formerly.

FIGURE 4-6

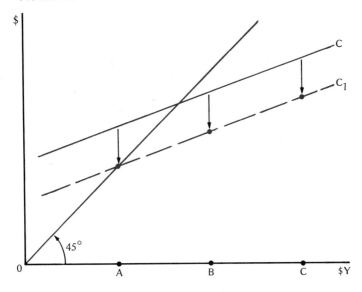

Try to explain to yourself the reverse case—where a desire to consume MORE will shift the consumption schedule up to C_2 (See Figure 4–7).

FIGURE 4-7

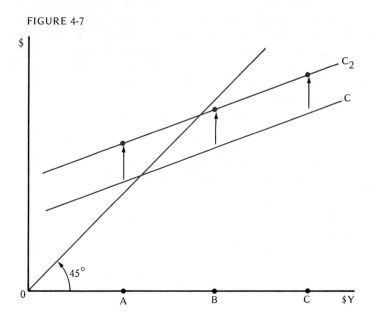

There is one final point to make on this topic, and it is an important one: many years of study on the spending and saving habits of the public give fairly convincing proof that the consumption and saving schedules do NOT tend to move up or down very much. Perhaps this is due to the fact that spending habits are ingrained and do not change very quickly, or perhaps it is because there is no necessary reason for any of the non-income determinants of consumption, just discussed, to all change in the same direction. For instance #1 might move in the direction of "more consumption" while at the same time #5 might alter in the direction of "more saving." In this case the two might well cancel each other out, leaving the consumption schedule about where it had been before.

INVESTMENT

Having discussed Consumption and Saving, a look can now be taken at the last of the key factors in the Keynesian theory— Investment.

In the last chapter we saw that investment occurs when businessmen construct new capital—plant and equipment, for example—in the effort to increase future output.

What is it that leads businessmen to invest? The answer lies in the net profit, that is, the revenue earned from going through with the new investment project, minus all the costs of the project. If when all costs are taken into account, including the cost of borrowing the money to finance the project, the businessman *still* expects to make a profit, then there will be a tendency for him to go through with his plans.

To leave it here, however, would be too simple, for there are a number of determinants which *affect* the net profitability of an investment project.

First, the expected cost of an undertaking may vary over time in a number of ways. The interest rate on borrowed funds has a proclivity to change in a modern economy; in the US over the last ten years, it has gone up quite a bit. Any time borrowed money costs more, a businessman will rightly expect less profit from an investment project than he would otherwise earn with a lower interest rate. Costs can also be affected by changes in the initial price of the capital goods themselves. Most machines or factories now have a higher building cost than they did ten years ago, and this will have to be considered by the businessman. Another cost is the expense of operating new capital equipment once it is built (fuel, hiring labor, insurance, etc.), plus the need to keep the capital in a good state of repair (spare parts, maintenance men, etc.). Finally, the real cost of an investment project may alter if new technological discoveries occur which make capital more productive. A new innovation which allows a machine to turn out 1000 doughnuts an hour has an obvious advantage over an old machine which could only turn out 800 but which cost the same to purchase.

A second factor which determines the level of investment is the businessman's *expectation* of whether he will make a profit. This is very important. He cannot be CERTAIN after all, and he must thus use his ability (or intuition) to predict future business conditions. Any businessman who invests risks funds for some more or less lengthy period of time. If economic conditions worsen, he is the loser. Thus in planning new projects, an entrepreneur will be continually trimming his sails, buoyant in mood when the economy is buoyant, hauling back on his plans when the economy is slack. For like the ship captain who does not know the winds and hoists the wrong sails, the entrepreneur too has reefs awaiting him if he makes incorrect investment decisions—and on his map the reefs are labeled losses and possible bankruptcy.

Actually there are many economic and psychological factors which affect the businessman's expectations: government antitrust policy, price controls, wars and rumors of wars, taxes, weather (in agriculture), strikes, elections, as well as his more orthodox attempts to predict the state of business in the months ahead. It is not surprising that with so many disparate factors to consider, expectations have sometimes given an apparently capricious and fickle quality to investment decisions.

Economists have gone one step further from expectations, however, and have noted that investment appears also to depend on the present level of profits being earned. High profits may tend to promote decisions for more investment; low profits lead to curtailed plans for capital formation. In one sense this may be nothing more than expectations percolating once again in the businessman's mind. Good profits bring out the Pollyanna in us and lead us to optimistic predictions of the future. Poor present profits lead us to pessimism. However, there is more to it than that, because high profits can provide more funds which can be invested, while conversely low profits may not allow entrepreneurs to hold anything back for reinvestment in the company.[7]

SUMMARY

Thus, the level of investment is determined basically in the following way: an entrepreneur considers the *cost* of a project (including the interest cost of borrowing). He then weighs against that cost the expected *return* from the project. If the return exceeds the cost, so that a net profit remains, the entrepreneur will have an economic motive to undertake the investment. Where a company is forming capital out of its own profits, the latter will also be an important determinant of investment.

---

[7]*This is still a debatable issue among economists, but there is a consensus that as long as businesses do use part of their profits for investment, then the mechanism described here is likely to be important.*

This completes our discussion of the three keystones in the Keynesian framework: Consumption, Saving and Investment. The next chapter explores how the three combine to determine a country's national income and national product. This in turn will show whether a country will suffer from depression, from inflation, or with sound judgment and some good luck, from neither—a problem which lies at the heart of the New Economics.

Questions

1. What determines Consumption and Saving? Investment?
2. What is the Consumption Schedule?
3. What is the purpose of the 45° line in our figures?
4. Why is investment traditionally more volatile than consumption and saving?

5.

HOW INCOME IS DETERMINED: The Circular Flow in the Keynesian Framework

The last chapter discussed what determines consumption, saving and investment, and hinted that these three are of prime importance in the Keynesian framework. Our task is now to try to fit them together in a coherent way.

At this point we have reached the stage where we can take up the problem of what determines the level of national income and national product. In so doing, we may consider whether a country has so little income that factors of production are going unemployed—a state of depression— or whether income is so high that the economy is overheated and prices are rising—a state of inflation.

In this discussion two of the earlier simplifying assumptions will be retained: first, foreign trade will be ignored, and second, any discussion of government activities will be postponed a bit further.

INCOME DETERMINATION

Now to income determination, the major topic of this chapter. There are several ways to view income determination: many find it easiest via the so-called "circular flow" diagrams.

A circular flow diagram is a very, very simple picture or "model" of an operating economy, which tries to draw attention to the key relationships in the Keynesian theory, and thus allows the reader to focus on just those elements which are crucial to the determination of what level income or product will achieve.

Take the easiest sort of circular flow diagram, as in Figure 5–1, which assumes that all *production* is carried out in one sector of the economy, the BUSINESS sector. In order to undertake output, business must hire factors of production from the sector of the economy which supplies them. This is called the HOUSEHOLD sector. Assume further that all *consumption* in the economy is carried on by households.

FIGURE 5-1

HOUSEHOLD SECTOR	BUSINESS SECTOR
(consumes and supplies factors of production to business)	(produces and hires factors of production from households)

In Figure 5–2, the household sector is labeled "H" and the business sector "B." The whole picture is kept very simple by employing three more assumptions: first, households spend all their income on making purchases from business. For now, they will neither save nor have to worry about taxes. Second,

FIGURE 5-2

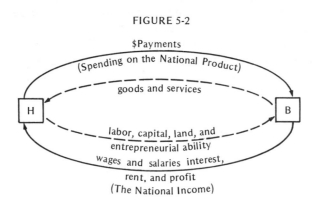

$Payments
(Spending on the National Product)
goods and services
H   B
labor, capital, land, and
entrepreneurial ability
wages and salaries interest,
rent, and profit
(The National Income)

business sells all that it produces—thus giving no problem of unsold goods piling up in inventory. Finally, business pays out to households all the money it receives as costs of production, the usual wages and salaries, rent and interest; and also pays out its profit to the entrepreneurs who run the businesses but are part of the household sector.

On the diagram note that business hires the factor of production from households and pays them their income. Meanwhile the households spend their income in order to buy the goods and services produced by business. Recall, as has been often repeated, the value of goods and services produced in the business sector is exactly equal to the income earned by households. Or, to put it another way, the spending on the goods produced by business is equal to the incomes that business pays out to have the goods produced (including profit).

In the simple world of the diagram, there is no reason why this cannot go on forever at the same rate. If business produces, say $1000 per year in goods and services, then it pays out $1000 as income to the factors of production: say $900 for land, labor and capital with $100 left over as profit for the entrepreneur. Thus the income of households is $1000 per year with which these same households carry on spending to the tune of $1000.

In very concise form we are now able to see *where* on the circular flow diagram the great money flows of the nation's economy are found. It should be completely clear that the bottom line represents the NATIONAL INCOME—that is the incomes earned by the factors of production—while the top line represents SPENDING ON THE NATIONAL PRODUCT. And they are here equal, as there are no leakages from nor injections to the circular flow: whatever business pays out as expenses plus the profit left over for entrepreneurs, business eventually receives back via the consumer spending of households.

Some of the assumptions made earlier in this chapter can now be relaxed. More realism is added by saying that NOT ALL of the incomes earned by households needs be spent on the goods and services produced by business. And perhaps NOT ALL the earnings received by business need be paid out as somebody's income. If this is agreed to, then there are two different types of subtractions from the circular flow, as seen in Figure 5–3.

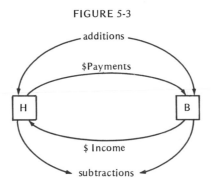

FIGURE 5-3

Also it might happen that additions to the inflows of the household sector take place over and above the sector's actual earnings, and that similar additions could bring other spending to business as distinct from the spending of consumers (also shown in Figure 5–3).

There are many types of subtractions from and additions to the circular flow, but it is sufficient to consider only a few of the important ones. First, take subtractions.

SUBTRACTION FROM THE CIRCULAR FLOW

As already stated, business pays incomes to the factors of production and this is in fact the national income. [Henceforth all the diagrams will be simplified, dealing only with the solid-line money flows, leaving off the dotted line real flows which show labor, land, capital and entrepreneurial ability flowing back to the business sector and goods flowing to the household sector.]

Earlier, something important was learned about this national income. It is commonly divided, as noted on page 31, into the different USES to which it might be put. With no government to worry about yet, there are only two such uses: CONSUMPTION and SAVING. Thus we can substitute for national income at the bottom of the circular flow the identical concept of C + S. (See Figure 5-4).

FIGURE 5-4

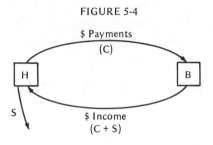

$ Payments
(C)

H

B

S

$ Income
(C + S)

How does this national income = C + S get disposed of on the circular flow diagram? One part of the answer is easy. For some time now we have been talking about the top portion of the circular flow, which represents spending by households on the goods and services produced by business. This is, then, consumption spending or just plain consumption (C)—the C which is earned below, and is spent above.

What about the rest of the national income? That would have to be the saving portion (S). Saving is a subtraction from the circular flow, because to the extent that anything is saved, it does not get spent for consumption. To put it another way, if people save then they MUST spend less than they have earned as income.

It is quite true that some or most of this saving may eventually find its way back into the circular flow if the savings are placed in banks, and then the banks make loans to businesses. Or, it may not find its way back in if banks do not want to loan, if businessmen do not want to borrow, or if people do not put their money in banks, but like Silas Marner put their trust in hiding places such as a wall safe, an old mattress, a hole in the floor.

Business firms, too, can save. When a company earns profit, some of it might not become available to households, because instead it is put aside as "undistributed profits," that is, the saving of businesses.

This also might quickly be put back into the circular flow if the saving is placed in banks which lend out the money; or if business turns right around and uses its own saving to construct new factories and so forth; but on the other hand as above it is possible that the funds would not find their way back into the flow.

In any case saving will be considered in itself a subtraction from the circular flow, whether carried on by households or businesses.

ADDITION TO THE CIRCULAR FLOW

Now to additions. Heretofore an important part of total spending has been omitted from the circular flow in that businessmen also contribute to total spending by undertaking investment on capital (new plant and equipment, etc.).

When money is spent for investment purposes (often it comes as a loan from a bank, but may come from other sources as well) the new investment means that SOME BUSINESS must receive new spending. Whoever builds the factory, constructs the machine, grades the railroad has to be the recipient of a money inflow, and note that this inflow forms an addition to the circular flow; that is, it does not stem from the consuming public in the household sector of the economy. (See Figure 5–5.)

FIGURE 5-5

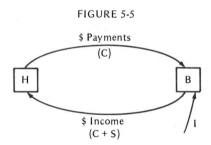

The fact that this additional spending takes place will in turn increase the quantity of the factors of production that businessmen will want to employ, and will therefore increase household income C + S (the bottom part of the flow).

Thus we have covered the two major items in total spending: consumer spending (C) and investment spending (I).

EQUILIBRIUM BETWEEN TOTAL OUTPUT AND TOTAL SPENDING

Now we are prepared to answer the central, vital question of the New Economics. Will there be sufficient total spending available in the economy so that business can meet all the costs of producing the economy's goods and services, including a reasonable profit?

What is the cost of producing an economy's goods and services in terms of the circular flow diagram? Recall that it is exactly equal to what is paid out—wages and salaries, rent, interest, profit: in other words the national income. Recall too that the national income can also be identified by finding what people intend to do with their earnings, which is either to consume or save. Thus C + S, consumption plus saving, is equivalent to the total cost of production, including profit, for an economy.

What in turn makes up total spending? As discussed above, that is spending on consumption plus spending for investment, which we have written C + I. The complete diagram of the circular flow is as shown in Figure 5-6.

FIGURE 5-6

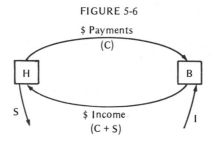

One situation can be foreseen in which businessmen as a whole will be satisfied with the overall relationship between their total cost of production (including a reasonable profit for them) and the spending that is directed toward the goods they produce. That feeling of satisfaction with the present state of affairs will occur when their costs and profit, that is, what is actually paid out by business to produce the nation's output C + S is exactly equal to the amount of spending that businessmen receive when they sell the goods and services they produce (which is, as noted above, C + I).

When all this is true, then C + S must equal C + I, a cardinal rule of the Keynesian economics. For there to be no general tendency for an economy to change because business-men in general are satisfied with the overall economic situation, then total spending C + I must equal total output and the income paid out to produce this output C + S. (Shown in Figure 5–7.)

FIGURE 5-7

$$\text{Total Income} = \text{Total Spending}$$
$$C + S = C + I$$

Now assume that for whatever reason you can think of, the total level of the nation's output has risen.[1] If this has occurred, it means in turn that income payments in terms of wages and salaries, interest, rent and profit have gone up as businessmen pay for the greater output, and thus it is automatically true that there is more available for the two purposes to which the national income is put: consumption and saving. So both C and S can be pictured as having increased.

Also assume, on the side of planned spending in the economy, that investment does not change at all but stays exactly where it was before.[2] In terms of spending, we have just said that C goes up, so that is already taken care of. This economy will show a higher C and a higher S on the side of income, and a higher C BUT A CONSTANT I on the side of spending. In our simple algebra, therefore, the higher C plus the higher S must be greater than the higher C plus the constant I. (This is shown in Figure 5–8.)

FIGURE 5-8

$$\text{Income} > \text{Spending}$$
$$C\uparrow + S\uparrow > C\uparrow + I$$

---

[1] For example, new productive innovations may have been put into service, or labor skills improved.

[2] This is another grand simplification, because in chapter 4 it was seen that business conditions (the level of output) will have an effect, perhaps substantial, on the level of investment. However, the simplification will allow a method of dealing with problems to be developed, after which, in the next chapter, investment will be allowed to rise as output rises.

The situation at this point is as follows: the total costs to businessmen of producing the greater quantity of output associated with a higher national income C + S is MORE than the total spending being received back by businesses in terms of C + I. To repeat, total costs paid out, which can be written C + S, exceed the total spending received back again as C + I.

What is the result of this? There will certainly be a reaction by businessmen, because firms *cannot be selling all they produce.* IF the value of production is higher than the amount of spending directed toward the purchase of that production, then it must be the case that some goods are going unsold.

What would therefore be occurring in the economy? As a general rule, an observer would find inventories piling up in the stores as goods remain unsold.

This leads to the important question: what further reaction would take place; what policy would business follow to stop the steady accumulation of unwanted goods? To stop this piling up of inventories, business firms will very naturally come to the decision that they must cut back on their level of total output.

When total output or production declines, note that this means something for C, S and I. The first result will be that as output is cut, total costs of production are reduced—and that is the exact same thing as saying that the incomes received by the factors of production (the national income) are reduced too. Recall that the national income is written as C + S. Both C and S would be expected to fall. (See Figure 5–9).

FIGURE 5-9

$$\text{Income} = \text{Spending}$$
$$C\downarrow + S\downarrow = C\downarrow + I$$

What about the side of spending? The last paragraph said that C had fallen; but by assumption I stayed the same. Where does this tendency to decline come to an end? Only where total production, that is, C + S, has been reduced to the point where there is sufficient spending available to buy all the goods offered for sale in the market, that is, where the lower C plus the lower S become EQUAL to the reduced C plus the constant I. In that case, again, C + S = C + I and again the economy returns to a balanced position.

The reader should be able, fairly rapidly, to turn the whole example around and ask himself what would be expected to happen if, starting from a position of balance, for any reason whatsoever the level of total output falls off.

If production is reduced, this will automatically mean what? That less is being earned in terms of wages, salaries, interest, rent, and profit. Or, said another way, the national income is down by the value of the decreased total output. In turn the lowered income means that people will plan lower consumption and lower saving, C + S.

As before, assume that the level of investment remains unchanged. On Figure 5–10 note the following: the lower C and the lower S, when added together, must be less than the lower C plus the constant I, and at the heart of the matter, it must be true that the nation's spending is greater than its output.

FIGURE 5-10

$$\text{Total Income} < \text{Total Spending}$$
$$C\downarrow + S\downarrow < C\downarrow + I$$

The result, as might be expected, is the exact opposite of the earlier case. With more spending than output, businessmen would notice in general a depletion of their inventories. To remedy this steady reduction, and to cash in on the potentiality for increased earnings that is offering itself, the managers of business firms will see to it that more productive factors are hired, and that total output is increased. The pressure, then, is a distinct one toward growing national product and national income.

Again the crucial point: how far does this growth in output and income continue before the pressure slackens? The answer: up to the point where a growing C and a growing S will once more equal a growing C but a constant I (as in Figure 5–11). For then, with C + S equal to C + I, there is no reason

FIGURE 5-11

$$C\uparrow + S\uparrow = C\uparrow + I$$

to expect a general tendency for inventories to be depleted any longer, because there is now a sufficient amount of production to match the total spending in the economy. So here again a state of balance is reached or, as economists use the term,

EQUILIBRIUM in the economy, and until something comes along to disturb that balance the economy will be under no tendency to alter its position with regard to income and output.

SUMMARY

Thus, at the center of the Keynesian New Economics is the idea that output will expand due to the perfectly logical actions of businessmen when total output and hence income C + S is less than aggregate spending C + I, until the point where their inventories stop decreasing and equilibrium is attained. Conversely, output will contract when output, hence income C + S, is greater than total spending C + I, to the point where inventories cease accumulating and a state of equilibrium is reached.

It is very important that this be fully understood; and in the next chapter this same conclusion will be reached in a different way.

Questions

1. What relationship do the household sector and the business sector have to each other in the "circular flow"?
2. How do additions to and subtractions from the circular flow affect its operation?
3. What happens when C + S is greater than C + I? When C + S is less than C + I? When C + S is equal to C + I?
4. What do business inventories have to do with the Keynesian framework?

6.

HOW
INCOME
IS
DETERMINED:
Other Ways of Looking
at Equilibrium

In the last chapter, the concept of equilibrium was explored. There are some alternate ways, however, in which this idea— so important to the New Economics—can be illustrated.

Rather than use circular flow data we will use some simple arithmetic. In Table 6–1 the reader will see five columns of data. Although the numbers are imaginary, they are designed to give a simple picture of equilibrium from a different vantage point.

EQUILIBRIUM: ARITHMETIC LOGIC

In column A, there are five different hypothetical levels of output—national product if you will. Either gross or net national product could have been selected; here the net figure is used. The various levels of output run from a low of $400 billion to a high of $800 billion.

Columns B and C show the planned consumption and the planned saving that is associated with each level of output. Naturally, since it has been shown that output is equal to income and since all income must be consumed or saved, then column B plus column C will always equal the total shown in column A.

Column D shows the level of intended investment and, as when considering the circular flow, the aim is for simplicity and the assumption is that planned investment is always a constant figure, say $60 billion, as shown.[1]

TABLE 6–1 *

A	B	C	D	E(=A)	F(=B+D)
Net National Product	Planned Consump- tion	Planned Saving	Planned Investment	Outpayments incurred by business = net national product	Planned spending on output of business = business receipts
(ALL IN BILLIONS OF DOLLARS)					
400	360	40	60	400	420
500	450	50	60	500	510
600	540	60	60	600	600
700	630	70	60	700	690
800	720	80	60	800	780

*This type of table has been long used in Paul Samuelson's textbook, Economics. See 8th edition, p. 213.

Column E lists the outpayments incurred by business to produce the national product (which, as pointed out earlier will include profit, which accrues to the entrepreneur). Remember that this figure, the cost of producing the nation's output, must also be the income that is received by the factors of production engaged in producing the output—that is the national income. To sum up, business expense to produce the national product is the national income, and that in turn is equal to another column in the table: column A, which shows net national product. We should recall that national product and national income are the same if we do not have to consider the government.

Column F can be termed the planned spending on the output of business, or alternately the receipts of business. Here is the heart of the problem—how much spending will flow back to business? Already the components of this figure are shown elsewhere in the table, for the two elements in spending, as stated many times now, are consumption (column

_____

[1]This assumption can be dropped with no major change in the analysis, as in footnote number 4 of this chapter.

B) and investment (column D). Thus C + I (column B + column D) = column F (planned spending).

Examine the situation described by this table carefully. Note that where planned spending is greater than output, for example at output level 400, spending 420, purchases are greater than production, an observer will expect business inventories to decline, and the tendency will be for business to *expand* its level of output. Note how this also holds true at the higher output level, 500. Again, spending *on* production is greater than the production itself, the outcome has to be a decline in business inventories, and there is equally a tendency for output to increase as in the first case.

But consider higher income levels, 700 or 800 for example. Given this state of affairs, the level of output in both cases exceeds the amount of spending that people are willing to undertake. Here, what will be the result? A portion of production will remain unsold, that is, business inventories will tend to increase, and the business sector must be under pressure to reduce its planned level of output.

ONLY AT A LEVEL OF OUTPUT EQUAL TO 600 is there a sufficient amount of spending so that there is neither a general shortage nor a general glut of goods. At this point, total spending equals total output, or to put it in other terms, there is sufficient aggregate demand C + I to buy up the nation's aggregate supply which we can write C + S. Only in this case will inventories neither expand nor contract, and it follows directly from this statement that only in this case will there be no overall tendency for businessmen to increase or decrease their total output.

Here, then, is EQUILIBRIUM in the context of the New Economics, this time not using directly the circular flow diagram, but instead relying on the arithmetic logic of the table.

EQUILIBRIUM: THE LOGIC OF DIAGRAMS

There is a third and final way to go about our search for equilibrium in the Keynesian sense, which utilizes the concept of the consumption schedule developed in chapter 4. This method is a little more sophisticated, but it possesses some helpful features not encountered in the first two explanations. It involves our old acquaintance the *consumption schedule* with investment added to it.

Remember that a schedule for consumption can be drawn showing that people plan to consume more as income increases, as in Figure 6–2.[2] However, this time investment is

FIGURE 6-2

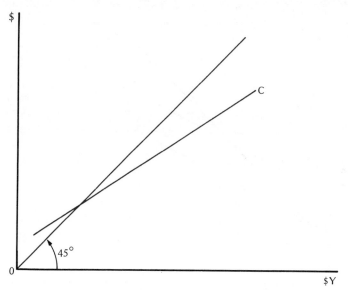

added to the diagram (see Figure 6–3). As before, the assumption is that the level of investment planned by businessmen is always equal to 60 no matter what the level of national income. In order to find the total level of spending in the economy at any level of income, all that must be done is to add the vertical distance 60 on top of the consumption schedule at every point along it, thus giving a new schedule which is consumption *plus* investment, or C + I. Note now that the C + I discussed in the past few chapters can be viewed *directly*—allowing a glance to reveal total spending at any level of income, or to use the equally acceptable alternate term, aggregate demand at any income level.

Now consider this diagram a little more closely. Recall what is involved in the innocent 45° line, so-called because it slopes outward from the zero-point origin of the graph at an angle of

---

[2]*As before, the letter Y stands for "income."*

45 degrees. In chapter 4 we saw that the difference between the consumption schedule C and the 45° line represents, at any level of income shown on the horizontal axis, that portion of income which people choose not to spend for consumption; that is, what they wish to save. For instance, at income level OB on Figure 6–3 people want to save the dollar amount XY.

FIGURE 6-3

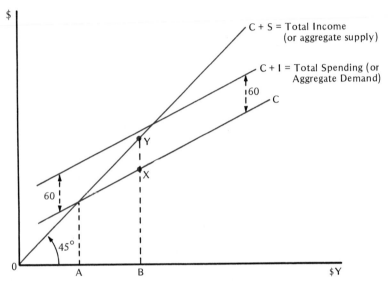

However, at income OA they don't want to save anything; their level of earnings is simply too low.[3] One thing should be fairly evident about all this: the 45° line at any point also represents C + S; it has to if consumption is measured vertically up to the C schedule while the difference between C and the 45 degree line is equal to S. So, to repeat, the 45° line also shows C + S at any level of income. And what *is* C + S? With government omitted, it is the national income (as all you can do with your income is consume or save) which in turn is exactly equal to the national product—the value of the goods and services produced in the economy. It is thus perfectly reasonable to call the 45° line aggregate supply —for that is indeed what it represents, a measure of all goods and services produced during a period of time.

Consider why this way of picturing equilibrium offers some

---

3 *At any income level lower than OA, there is dissaving, with people drawing down their level of accumulated past savings.*

advantages not encountered before. For one thing, we can see directly on this diagram whether or not there is too little spending C + I or too much, at any income, to purchase the nation's output. The point on which to focus attention is the place where the lines cross: because only there, where the C + I schedule intersects the 45° line, does C + S = C + I. This has been all along our condition for equilibrium. Only there will there occur no increase or decrease in business inventories, thus generating no pressure for changes in total output. Thus, on Figure 6–4, the national income at which total spending C + I is equal to total output C + S is labeled "E" for equilibrium.

FIGURE 6-4

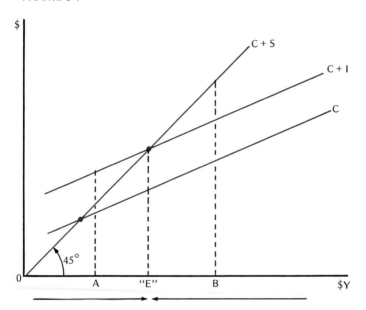

At output level OA, on the other hand, spending C + I can be seen to exceed output C + S. With spending greater than output, inventories are depleted and production is pressured upward toward E by the actions of businessmen.

Conversely, what if income should be at the much higher level OB? There output C + S exceeds C + I spending. Total spending less than total output must mean rising inventories in the business community, and pressure developing to contract total output and hence national income toward E.

So at long last the analysis has been completed, with our path taking us through three different methods—the circular flow charts, the arithmetical examples, and the diagrams. For some, this threefold exploration may be overly repetitious, but the concept of equilibrium is so essential to the New Economics that it requires full understanding.[4]

---

[4]An alteration in the diagram must be made if, as discussed earlier, the level of present investment is not always a constant. We have already seen that the amount of investment being carried on at any time is likely to depend on business expectations of what future income will be (see page 42). A high national income now may therefore stimulate investment because businessmen foresee a rosy future; but a low income and the discouraging outlook which accompanies it may well depress investment. If all this is so, the C + I line can be slightly modified to show I rising as national income is larger. On Figure 6–5, I diverges steadily from C at higher income levels. But the analysis of equilibrium remains the same. The reader can make this adjustment if he so wishes in any of the diagrams used henceforth.

FIGURE 6-5

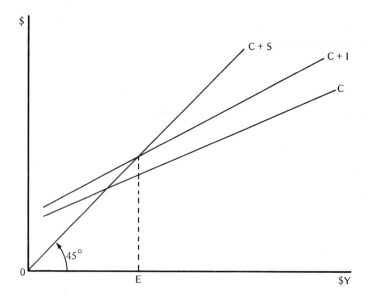

Appendix

"THE CLASSICAL FALLACIES"

With the knowledge gained in the foregoing chapter of equilibrium and how it is attained, it is possible to take up a problem met with in chapter 1 but a more complete discussion of which had to be postponed because the analytical tools necessary for an understanding of its implications had not yet been developed.

Chapter 1 discussed how the classical economists—that hardy breed which started with Adam Smith in 1776 and headed the field for over a century and a half—believed faithfully that extended inflations or depressions could not occur. In the terms of chapter 6, they thought an economy would never lack sufficient spending to purchase all output. This trust was based on "Say's Law," named after the French economist J. B. Say.[5] In simplified fashion, Say's Law states that "supply creates its own demand." Basically, the classicists theorized that when output was produced, the same amount of income was generated which, in turn, would then be spent in buying the output on the market. Thus underspending, leading to depression, would not take place.

The only possible flaw in this logic was that people might want to save a different amount from what businessmen wished to invest, which COULD make spending $(C + I)$ differ from output and income $(C + S)$. But the classicists replied, no, saving and investment would not differ because there is a trustworthy mechanism which will ensure that $S = I$. They believed that the interest rate would always work to equalize the two, and thus force spending always to equal output.

How would this operate? The classicists assumed that businessmen's investment plans are dictated by the interest rate. If they have to pay a great deal to borrow, they will not be tempted to do so. However, low interest rates will stimulate investment. They also thought that savers are primarily

---

[5]As Thomas Balogh put it, "Economic theory was, for a century, completely hoaxed" by Say's Law. See his Unequal Partners, The Theoretical Framework, vol. I (Oxford: Basil Blackwell, 1963), p. 1.

motivated by the interest they earn on savings. A high rate, more saving; a low rate, reduced saving.

The classicists believed interest was the automatic regulating mechanism which would keep saving equal to investment. The mechanism was supposed to work as follows: say interest rates are high, perhaps 8%. What then? People will want to save a great deal, but businessmen will certainly not be tempted to invest very much. All this will have an impact on the banking system, where the classicists felt savings would be kept on deposit and where the funds to finance investment would be borrowed. Banks see they are attracting more savings than businessmen want to borrow. So they will lower the interest rate. Perhaps to 4%. Then what? Businessmen are much more inclined to borrow at that figure, of course, but people do not have their former motivation to save. So banks are thronged with customers wanting loans but do not attract enough savings. The result is that they raise the interest rate. Finally a rate is arrived at, say 6%, at which savers want to save just the amount that businessmen want to borrow. This is the mechanism by which saving would always equal investment. Symbolically $S = I$ and with $C = C$, then spending $(C + I)$ must always be equal to output $(C + S)$. The economy is thus always in a state of equilibrium.

Where did the classicists go wrong? For one thing, as already discussed in chapter 4, they were wrong in believing that the interest rate plays the major role in determining what people want to save. It doesn't. Instead, the level of income is much more important.

More significant and in fact destructive to the classical analysis, is that while businessmen do consider the rate of interest when investing, their final aim is profit, and if they see the public spending less and saving more, this means sales are dropping. In a climate of declining sales it is senseless to think that lower interest rates caused by the increase in saving will persuade entrepreneurs to invest more. With consumer spending plummeting all around them, it is conceivable that even with extremely cheap borrowed money, with a near-zero rate of interest, businessmen still will not want to invest if commercial prospects are so bad.

Still, the classical economists thought they had a guarantee of equilibrium in Say's Law. They were therefore convinced that a capitalist economy would be inherently very stable.

Going one step further, the classicists depended upon another theory to assure that the state of their very stable economy would be one of the full employment of the factors of production. No men who wanted to work would go without work, no machines would stand idle, no useful land and buildings would go unused. This was the "law of wage and price flexibility." Should an economy find itself in a depression for any reason, according to this theory the situation would be automatically corrected. Unemployment of labor would force wages down; unemployment of machines, land, etc., would force their prices down too. Businessmen, seeing the new low rates, would take the opportunity to hire the previously unemployed labor, machines, land, etc. In short, depressions (and inflations, if the logic used above is reversed) would be automatically self-correcting.

The Law of Wage and Price Flexibility sounds very convincing, but unfortunately, economic evolution tended to bypass it almost completely. For example, the existence of strong unions, minimum-wage legislation, and extreme public dislike of wage cuts all meant that wages in particular were not nearly as flexible as was originally assumed. Even more important, even if wages fell drastically, would that not mean that the purchasing power of the greatest part of the population was cut? And would not a drop in purchasing power appear to businessmen as a worsening of economic conditions? Instead of hiring the unemployed at their new lower wages, businessmen might well be tempted to cut back output still further. Such was the sad story during the Great Depression.

Thus the two-fold classical mechanism was not reliable.[6] Lord Keynes argued that it be replaced with a new system, and that system is discussed in the next chapter.

---

[6]It need hardly be pointed out that the sudden demise of a whole theoretical framework will spark enormous controversy, and that is quite true of both Say's Law and Wage-Price Flexibility. This appendix reflects the orthodox opinion, but there are many variants. Especially with wage-price flexibility, where the 20th century has shown growing "stickiness" in BOTH wages and prices, is there much debate of whether the argument might hold water under some special circumstances. (See more advanced texts for further discussion.)

Questions

1. How do the circular flow charts, the arithmetic example, and the "C + I" diagram, come to the same conclusion?
2. What happens when total spending exceeds total output? Vice-versa?
3. What is meant by equilibrium?
4. Why did the classical economists feel that an economy would be inherently stable at full employment? Where did they go wrong?

7.

HOW
INCOME
IS
DETERMINED:
The Keynesian Framework
Completed

This chapter concludes our discussion of equilibrium in the New Economics, that is, the pressures which tend to change the level of national income and which arise from the relationship between total spending and total output. The consumption schedule "C" ought now to be very familiar; recall that it shows how much the public wants to consume, and hence to save, at any level of income. In the background, lying behind the level of consumption, are a fairly large number of underlying conditions. These may change, and thus directly influence the decisions people make concerning consumption and saving.

FACTORS CHANGING CONSUMPTION AND INVESTMENT SPENDING

A list was presented in chapter 4 of various non–income items which might affect the level of consumption and saving. These items included stocks of liquid assets, the quantity of durable goods on hand, future expectations of prices and incomes, the level of debt, and the public's attitude toward thrift.

When any of these underlying conditions changes, an alteration in people's spending and saving habits must take place. If people are more concerned with old age, for example, they will as a whole decide to save a greater amount from their earnings whether income is high or low. Any such change can be pictured on a diagram, using the consumption schedule of the past few chapters.

For example, the increase in saving mentioned above would be shown by moving the consumption schedule downward, implying that less consumption is intended at any level of income, and vice-versa for a decrease in saving. Naturally, a reduction in "C" automatically reduces C + I. (See Figure 7–1).

FIGURE 7-1

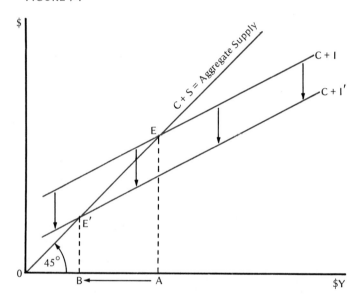

Investment might also be subject to changing conditions not associated with the present level of national income. One important case, mentioned already, might be an alteration in the rate of interest, where a decline would tend to lead to more investment, a rise to less investment. Or expectations of the future may change. A belief that business will boom would be expected to cause an increase of investment at any level of income; the pall of gloom when expectations are uniformly bad would be expected to lead to a decline in the amount of investment anticipated. An increase in the level of investment planned by business is shown in the same way as an increase in planned consumption: simply move the C + I schedule vertically upward all along its length. (Figure 7–2).

FIGURE 7-2

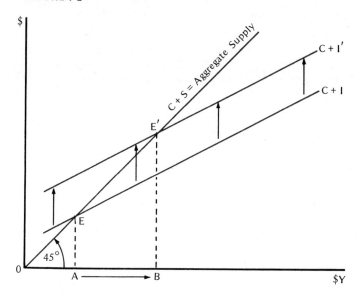

These movements, logical and easy, seem innocent enough to the uninitiated; but there is a very important lesson to be garnered here. Whenever the position of C + I is moved upward or downward due to an alteration in the desire to consume, or in the desire to save[1] or in businessmen's plans to invest, then any one of these will CHANGE THE POINT OF EQUILIBRIUM.

If people want to save more and consume less, to take our earlier example, this is shown on a consumption plus investment diagram by a decline in total spending C + I, and the downward movement in the C + I schedule will auto-matically change the equilibrium point from what it was before to the new point where the altered C + I crosses the 45° line. For only at that new position will total spending C + I be equal to total output and hence income C + S. Note that exactly the same thing would be true if, for any reason, businessmen decided that at any level of national income they wanted to invest less.

Take the other side of the coin. Should planned

---

[1]*Note again that saving is simply what is left over after consumption takes place, as what is not consumed is saved.*

consumption increase for any reason, no matter what the level of income (that might be due to the belief that prices will soon be going up, or a surge in the number of people who believe in "Keeping up with the Joneses") OR should planned investment increase, or both, then total spending has risen and there has to be an increase in the equilibrium position of national income.

Any way you look at it, a movement in C (or S) or a movement in I MUST cause a change in equilibrium.[2]

FULL EMPLOYMENT

At this point we come to an important consideration of equilibrium—vital to a comprehension of the New Economics —and so particular attention should be directed to what follows. Note that up to now there has been no mention of where depression and inflation fit into all this. The connection lies in how high the level of national income is. Presume that somewhere along the horizontal axis of one of the figures, (see 7–3), there is a dollar amount of national income just large enough so that there is full employment. Be careful to realize that up to now nothing has been said about where that point is—our whole discussion on equilibrium had to do with where the national income would tend to go, NOT whether there would be full employment at that point.

So, as just stated, somewhere there will be a level of national income which is just sufficiently large so that everyone who wants to work has a job, and factories, machines, and so forth are all occupied and running to capacity. This is shown at the point marked "full employment."

---

[2]An important point, taken up in detail in more advanced texts, is that a change in C, or S, or I, will actually cause national income to change by a numerically greater quantity. This can clearly be seen on both diagrams 7–1 and 7–2, where the movement in C + I is far less than the fall in income AB (7–1) or the rise in income AB (7–2). This phenomenon is called the theory of the "multiplier." It is caused by the re-spending of consumption or investment dollars in the following manner: if a businessman invests by building a new $100 machine, someone or some group receives $100 in new income for their labor, raw materials, etc. But these income recipients will in turn spend some of their additional income (also saving some of it) so that national income is raised by more than the original investment.

FIGURE 7-3

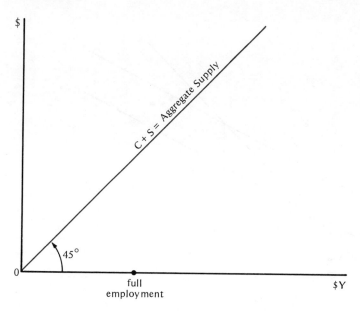

What if income is *lower* than this? Of necessity any lower amount must mean there is insufficient production going on in the economy to bring about the full employment of all the men and other factors of production that are willing to work. One encompassing and familiar word for this state of affairs is depression.

Conversely, it is possible that national income will be *higher* than that which would produce full employment for the economy. One thing is certain: when employment is full, it will not be possible to obtain more goods and services even if national income should move to the right of this point along the horizontal axis of the diagram. To say it another way, if the equilibrium point shows that national income is higher than what can actually be attained with the economy at full employment, then the only way that the national income could be made higher would be a general rise in the price level—inflation. That is why on Figure 7–4, the entire

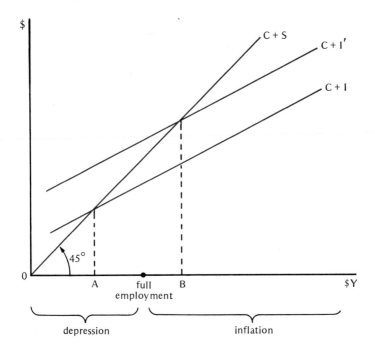

FIGURE 7-4

horizontal axis located to the right of that national income which would give full employment must be the region of inflation.

Be quite certain that you understand the full implications of these two areas, depression to the left of the all-important full employment point and inflation to the right. Depending on where the C + I schedule intersects the 45° line, the position of equilibrium could be anywhere in the diagram. The rule then has to be that EQUILIBRIUM (C + S = C + I) does not at any time or in any way guarantee that the economy is at full employment.

Recall the concept of equilibrium: that level of national income toward which the economy tends because of the vital relationship between total output and total spending. But equilibrium can certainly be at OA on Figure 7–4 where it has quite clearly left the country stuck in a depression. Historical evidence demonstrates that capitalism had to put up with centuries of economic slumps which followed fairly regularly, one after another. In the terms of this chapter, the point of equilibrium showed where the economy was tending, but that final resting place was too often one of depression.

The converse can be readily shown, as at OB on the same diagram. As before, should total spending C + I intersect the 45° line above the position of full employment, then national income must indeed be under pressure to move toward the higher level. But it was pointed out above that a higher national income than can be obtained at full employment is an illusion which can be reached only through a general rise in prices, that is, inflation.

Or, to top it all off, there is no reason why by chance—or we can give it more emphasis and say by the merest coincidence—equilibrium could not occur AT full employment, with total spending C + I crossing the 45° line just at that level of national income which ensures that all men and other factors of production that want a job will in fact get work.

The point remains, however, that there is no NECESSARY relation between full employment and equilibrium at all— perhaps the major point made by Lord Keynes and the New Economists in their criticism of the classical theory engendered by the experience of the Great Depression of the 1930's.

A brief resume might be helpful here. The classical economists felt certain that the public need not worry about long bouts with inflation and depression because of their two-fold mechanism ensuring that they would not occur. Both parts of the classical theory were examined when the flexibility of wages and other prices, and Say's Law—supply creates its own demand—were discussed in the appendix to chapter 6. But Keynes and his followers were able to explain where both these theories had gone astray and to show that unfortunately for everybody concerned, and especially for the labor force, equilibrium is divorced from full employment as a concept. An economy will tend toward a certain position, to be sure, but the movement is governed by the equality of total spending and total output, NOT by their relationship to full employment without inflation. This is the most important single fact contained in the first part of this book.

DEFLATIONARY AND INFLATIONARY GAPS

Economists often, and the news media sometimes, use specific terms to describe the state of affairs when the equilibrium level of national income is either above or below the point where national income would give full employment without inflation.

Two examples will demonstrate how this terminology is used. First of all, take the case where national income is in equilibrium at a point noticeably below the full employment level–marked OEd on Figure 7–5, using the "d" to indicate a climate of depression.

FIGURE 7-5

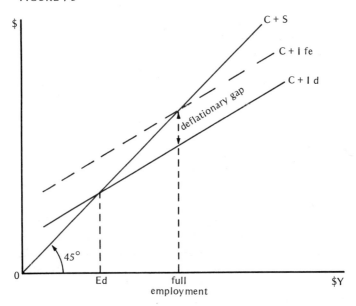

Notice at this position OEd—caused of course by the intersection of C + I d with the 45° line—there must be some measurable rise in the C + I schedule, or total spending, which would bring it into intersection with the 45° line at the full employment level. This hypothetical rise, the distance between the old C + I which gave us an equilibrium below full employment, and some new C + I which will give non-inflationary full employment, can be marked off on the diagram, and this vertical distance—here the distance between C + I d and C + I fe (for full employment) is traditionally termed the DEFLATIONARY GAP.

It should be easy to do this all over again on the other side of full employment without inflation. Consider the case where equilibrium is located at a level of income higher than the critical full employment point, shown on Figure 7–6 as Ein, standing for inflation. Here, C + I in, crosses the 45° line to bring on inflation.

FIGURE 7-6

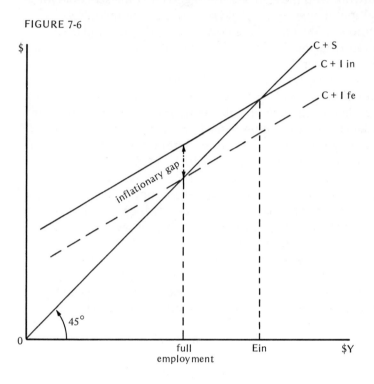

If this is so, there must be some measurable fall in total spending C + I which would give us a new equilibrium, again at non–inflationary full employment. This hypothetical fall, which can be marked off as the vertical distance between the old schedule for total spending, C + I in and some new schedule C + I fe, is known as the INFLATIONARY GAP.

Both the deflationary and the inflationary gaps must, as history shows, have been with us as long as market capitalism has been our system of economic organization. Both have been facts of life, though of course these names were not used until the Keynesian Revolution took place.

INTRODUCING THE GOVERNMENT

It is surely self-evident that a great task of the New Economics must be to eliminate both gaps whenever they occur, thus attempting the cure for inflation and depression which for so long eluded the most avid economists. How to eliminate them? Our work with these diagrams suggests that the schedule for total spending, C + I, should be manipulated by policy-decision on the part of the government, the manipulation obviously taking the form of closing inflationary or deflationary gaps whenever they should appear.

So the next step is to turn to the consideration of WHAT governmental policy could be used to close the gaps. Immediately one unfortunate circumstance having to do with the level of consumption raises its head. It has been found, from long experience, that consumption is notoriously not amenable to alteration. Like the Rock of Gibraltar, the consumption schedule seems to stand there on the same spot without changing by any great amount. Just asking people to change their habits of consumption (which, recall, automatically means they change their habits of saving as well) is no more successful than Spanish policy has been to get their flag hoisted over the real Rock of Gibraltar. There seem to be only a very few major exceptions to the general stability of the consumption schedule. One example is during a major war that has widespread popular support, such as World War II. Historically in such periods it has been possible to get some alteration in desired consumption by exhortation and widespread propaganda: for example, everyone in our plant must buy war bonds. (This, note, will shift the consumption schedule downward—less consumption and more saving at any level of income.) Patriotic messages of this type can be used at other times too. During the crisis of August, 1971, various government officials exhorted Americans to consume more.[3]

---

[3]During 1970–71 adverse economic conditions led people to consume slightly less and to save slightly more of their income. This was probably due to the high level of unemployment and the desire to increase savings as a protective measure. The government's appeals to alter this situation were apparently having little success, however.

Advanced works discuss more minor possibilities for short-term changes in consumption and saving.

INVESTMENT holds more hope for manipulation, because as has been seen, the interest rate is among the determining factors which establish how much investment will be undertaken.

Low interest rates tend to encourage investment and high rates to discourage it. Thus, if by policy decision interest rates could be lowered, it might be possible to push up the amount of investment that businessmen want to undertake, and vice-versa. In the next two chapters close attention will be focused on this possibility.

Fortunately for the New Economics, and for those whose desire it is to control the cycles of boom and slump that our country has traditionally undergone, there is another broader realm where governmental activity might be brought into play against the inflationary or deflationary gap. This area has been ruled out of our discussion for a number of chapters now—the spending and tax policies of federal, state, and local government.

Obviously the government does add to spending, heretofore limited in our analysis to C + I only; the government's own spending will surely have to be considered in addition to consumption and investment.

In terms of a diagram of the circular flow, first met in chapter 5 (see Figure 7–7), we can lead in a stream of government spending labeled G, and for the sake of simplicity in the diagram it will be assumed that all government spending is for the purchase of goods and services produced by the private business sector of the economy, B. TOTAL spending in the economy thus has a new item: our old consumption plus investment now augmented by government expenditure C + I + G.

FIGURE 7-7

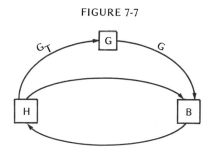

Even more obviously (and painfully), the government takes a portion of all incomes earned by households (the national income) as taxation. Earlier it was noted that the only two things you can do with the income you earn is to spend it on goods and services (consumption) or save it; but henceforth allowance must be made for the necessity of paying taxes to the government, Gt. Thus all income earned can be disposed of in three ways, and the national income will be equal to consumption plus saving plus the new item, government taxation, or $C + S + Gt$, which is simply a breakdown of the total figure for national income and output. (Of course government also taxes the business sector as well, but it will not change the logic of our argument to show all taxes on the diagram as paid by households.)

All this will undoubtedly affect our discussion of EQUILIBRIUM national income, but rest assured that the basic rule of thumb still holds. Equilibrium in the national income will occur where total output (and income, of course) equals total spending. Or in synonymous terms, aggregate supply equals aggregate demand. Thus the equilibrium condition is $C + S + Gt = C + I + G$.

FIGURE 7-8

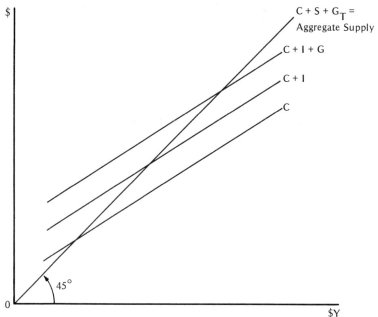

In terms of our schedules, all this can readily be shown by just adding another line. If government expenditure G is simply added on top of all other spending C + I, a new schedule for total spending results, which is C + I + G. (See Figure 7–8).

Remember that on a diagram of this type any level of national income and output is exactly equal to total spending at only one unique series of positions—along the 45° line. To the right of equilibrium, planned spending can be seen to be less than planned output; to the left planned spending exceeds planned output. The reasons why this situation cannot be permanent have already been discussed in past chapters and the logic is here identical. The addition of government makes no change whatever in the reaction of businessmen, as they see inventories declining when spending exceeds output, or when they see inventories accumulating when spending is less than output. In either case, they will be under pressure to change their production decisions and thus change the value of national output and income.

Thus a wide range of policy decisions presents itself. Because the government can raise or lower its expenditure G, thus seizing the opportunity actually to manipulate total spending C + I + G upward or downward, it can try to eliminate an inflationary or deflationary gap.

OR it can use, as a distinct act of policy, its power of taxation. If government raises taxes, there is clearly less income left to households for consumption, and less to business for investment. We can therefore expect higher taxes to push C + I + G down, lowering the equilibrium level of national income.

Then the reverse: if government *lowers* taxes, there is *more* income left to households for consumption and more to business for investment, so C + I + G *rises*, also raising the equilibrium level of national income.

That is how the government plays a role in the New Economics. Our task will henceforth be to explore these functions in detail.

Questions

1. What causes the equilibrium point to change?
2. What is the relationship between full employment and equilibrium?
3. What is an inflationary gap? A deflationary gap?
4. How does the addition of government alter the analysis?

8.

MONETARY POLICY:
Banks, Money and The Federal Reserve System

The last chapter completed our overview of the central theses of the New Economics, developing what was Lord Keynes' major contribution to economic doctrine as we know it today. His theory is in regular use throughout the world of market capitalism all the way from Australia to Sweden. At this, the halfway point of the book, it is time to note that in only two countries is there any great body of opinion which has failed to fully endorse the new theories: West Germany, where the problem is very largely a legal one caused by her somewhat unusual federal constitution written just after World War II, and our own country, the US, where the New Economics has tended to become a standard political issue.[1]

But the essence of the Keynesian theory stands above the give and take of partisan politics on its own logic. For if, as shown earlier, the equilibrium level of national income and output is established by the equality of planned spending

---

[1]This used to divide somewhat along party lines, with Democrats ordinarily Keynesian in their economics and Republicans ordinarily not. Nowadays, with President Nixon having stated in 1970 that he is a believer in the New Economics, the skeptics are located in lower echelons than they used to be. Nevertheless there are many vocal Americans in Congress and in the business world who have not fully accepted the analysis presented here.

with planned output, that is, aggregate demand and aggregate supply, then there is present a potentially powerful weapon for the *elimination* of the cycles of inflation and depression.

This weapon is the ability to *alter* the level of total spending, which is made up of consumption spending plus investment plus government spending $C + I + G$. (See Figure 8–1). This

FIGURE 8-1

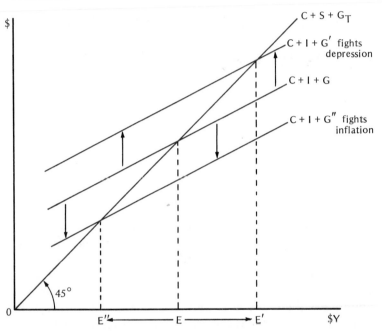

schedule—seen many times on graphs of the type shown here —will work to squeeze out inflationary gaps or deflationary gaps whenever they should develop, if it can be bodily shoved upward or downward, and if the policies of the New Economics are understood and correctly applied.[2]

---

[2]*It used to be hoped that inflationary and deflationary gaps might be eliminated completely by these Keynesian tools, but any literate reader knows that when, as in 1970–71, inflation has been running at about 5% and unemployment at about 6% in the US, this hope has not been borne out. With the early optimism dispelled, the most that can be said now is that the very large booms and slumps in the economy can be controlled within a fairly narrow range. Eliminating them entirely is a much tougher problem, one that is considered at length in chapter 14.*

GOVERNMENT: MONETARY POLICY

What are the ways available to manipulate aggregate demand
C + I + G? Recall that a direct change in consumption via
exhortation or propaganda is unlikely with the possible
exception of a major national emergency. But there remain
three ways in which the government DOES have the power
to alter these critical variables.

First is via the economy's structure of interest rates, which
can affect, perhaps decisively, the plans of businessmen as far
as investment is concerned. Second, government will have a
direct impact on C + I + G via its own spending. Any changes
in this will automatically raise or lower the whole schedule.
Finally, the same result can be obtained by the use of tax
policy, as tax increases will lower the amount left to the public
for consumption and to businessmen for investment, while
tax decreases will raise that amount, lowering and raising the
schedule respectively.[3]

In future chapters the latter two, that is, the government's
policies of spending and taxation, will have to be fully considered. For now, however, our concentration will be on the
first of these methods: altering interest rates via policy decision
to affect the level of planned investment. (And note in passing
that one other component of spending might be affected
by changes in the interest rate, since some of the spending of
state and local governments are quite dependent on the
amount that must be paid to borrow money. Thus part of G
in C + I + G will be affected by the argument.)

THE INTEREST RATE AND INVESTMENT

Working through the interest rate to control the level of
investment might be called the traditional method, because
the basic details, lumped together under the familiar term
MONETARY POLICY, have by and large been well-known
since *before* the birth of the New Economics. It dates from
actions taken by the Bank of England in the 19th century,

---

[3]*Note once again a point made in chapter 7 and called the "multiplier." Any
change in C, I, or G, will have an amplified impact on national income.*

and became familiar in the US just before and after World War I.

Monetary policy acts through the supply of money, as the name implies, to change interest rates and the plans of businessmen for investment.[4] The idea is that an increase in the supply of money, just as an increase in the supply of *any* good, is likely to cause a decrease in the price you must pay for it. Take potatoes: even youngsters are going to suspect that if a potato blight strikes Maine, then the resulting shortage of potatoes will cause their price to rise. It is the same with funds destined for investment. If businessmen borrow for investment purposes, the shorter the supply of money for loans, then the more they will have to pay to borrow.

If the government can arrange a CONTRACTION in the supply of money, the price of borrowing (the interest rate) will be expected to rise, and higher interest rates increase the cost of any investment project. The final result is that planned investment tends to decline.

On the other hand, if the government can *increase* the money supply, this will mean more funds available for lending; thus, interest rates decline, and investment is encouraged. So the government may be able to move the C + I + G schedule on the diagram one way or the other, simply by controlling the quantity of money available.

There was a time, as we hinted on page 83, when economists (and bankers) thought that this mechanism was of universal importance for all types of investment. Experience has shown, however, that some types of investment are far more sensitive than others to changes in the interest rate. For example, house construction is drastically affected by the cost of borrowed funds, because that cost is such a high percentage of the total. State and local government spending are also affected strongly, as are the plans of small businessmen who depend almost wholly on borrowed funds for investment. But in recent years a growing body of opinion has held that the interest rate does not affect the investment plans of big corporations nearly as much as it does the other areas just mentioned. One reason is that in a time of inflationary conditions with profit expectations high and growing, even

---

[4]*Or such is the aim. The mechanism does not always come up to the expectations of economists earlier in this century, for reasons to be immediately explained.*

hefty boosts in the interest rate may not concern corporate executives if they feel they can recoup these expenses from subsequent price increases for their goods. Then too, higher profits give the wherewithal for expanded investment, notwithstanding the interest cost on borrowed funds. Thus in what follows, the reader should be warned that monetary policy is likely to have a very selective, and not universal, impact.

MONEY AND NEAR-MONEY

Before the exploration of Monetary Policy begins, it is a very good idea to be completely clear on what is meant by the supply of money. This is not quite as easy as it sounds. Go out on the street and take a private poll, asking the question "What is money?" Though you will doubtless get a lot of agreement, you might miss something important. Everyone would concur on such items as coins and paper currency, such as the Federal Reserve notes in your wallet or the silver certificates which have now just about completely disappeared. But in reality, this is only a small part—about 20%—of the total supply of money. (See Figure 8–2.)

FIGURE 8-2

BANK DEPOSITS

$170 billion

PAPER MONEY
$43 billion

coins — $6 billion

As of early 1971

The remaining four-fifths, by far the most important part of the money supply, is made up of the common ordinary checking account, demand deposits as they are called because they are payable to the holder on demand. There are several other types of paper which are almost as negotiable as demand deposits. Savings deposits for example, or government bonds, or shares in a savings and loan association and so forth. All of these, however, require such things as a trip to the bank or working through a broker for cashing, which involves time, so they cannot truly be considered as part of the money supply. Instead, they are usually classified as NEAR-MONEY.[5]

We will omit any further discussion of Near-Money and instead concentrate on the main elements of the American money supply. These are coins and paper currency plus that most important item, demand deposits.

Almost everybody must suspect that the government has fairly direct control over the volume of coins and paper money that it can issue. This is quite true, but as we just mentioned this form of money is also relatively unimportant when compared to demand deposits. So some time will have to be spent carefully considering the question of what determines the volume of demand deposits and the additional and important point, do the authorities have any *control* over what the size of these deposits will be.

FEDERAL RESERVE SYSTEM

Investigation shows that *banks*—ordinary commercial banks—play the major role here. America has about 14,000 in all (there were many more 40 years ago before the Great Depression caused thousands to close their doors forever). They range in size from giants such as the country's biggest—the Bank of America with headquarters in San Francisco and assets of over 20 billion dollars—down to little village banks with assets of less than one ten-thousandth as much. It is interesting that the US is one of the few countries with many separate, individual banks. In Great Britain, for instance, the tourist will find only four or five big ones, like Midland's, Barclay's, and Lloyd's, with branch offices all over the country. The same thing is true of our neighbor, Canada.

Of the 14,000 American banks, about one-third are national

---

[5]*Economists, and increasingly the financial press, use the term "M_1" to describe the money supply as made up of coins plus paper currency plus demand deposits. "M_2" and "M_3" are used when the various forms of near money are included.*

banks, which means that they have obtained their charter of incorporation from the federal government. The other two-thirds are state banks, meaning that they have acquired *their* charter of incorporation from the state in which they operate.

All the national banks and about 15% of the state ones are members of that very important semi–independent branch of the government, which guards its autonomy with care, the Federal Reserve System (nicknamed the Fed).

In fact the importance of the Fed is much greater than the figures for membership imply. That is because the non-members, numbering a little over half of all American banks, are usually small in size. These nonmembers actually hold only about 17% of all demand deposits.

The Fed is this country's central bank, or government bank, and corresponds to such old and famous institutions as the Bank of England, the Bank of Canada, the Banque de France, and West Germany's Deutsche Bundesbank.

Unlike these, however, the Fed is not just one bank but 12, the 12 being located in each of the various Federal Reserve Districts, as for example, the Federal Reserve Bank of New York or the Federal Reserve Bank of Denver. The reason for the Fed's split personality is largely political. Long ago we had a central bank, the Bank of the United States in Philadelphia which operated during 1791–1811 and then again from 1816 to 1836. But the Bank of the United States ran afoul of President Jackson, a bad man to cross as the British found at the Battle of New Orleans, and it was legislated out of existence. Because of fears generated by those 19th century political battles, when a central bank was again considered in the first decade of this century it was thought wise to have its power somewhat lessened by the 12-way division that we live with today.[6]

All 12 banks have their own directors, but these are subservient to the seven members of the so-called Board of Governors, with headquarters in Washington. The members of the Board of Governors are appointed by the President for terms which last 14 years (long enough to assure a degree of independence for the Fed, especially since it is arranged that the terms are staggered so that no President is able to appoint

---

[6]*Several foreign central banks are much older. The Banque de France dates from 1800, the Bank of England from 1694.*

a block of members to the Board of Governors at the same time). The most important member of the seven is the Chairman of the Board of Governors, currently Arthur Burns, on whose shoulders rests the prime responsibility for announcing and explaining the management of the country's money supply. The Board is the chief administrative body of the Fed and has at its command several weapons which make up its arsenal of monetary policy.

HOW BANKS CREATE MONEY

One more task remains before taking up the intricacies of monetary policy. It will be necessary to discover how commercial banks create or destroy money—perhaps this will be a surprising statement to the uninitiated—for it is through the creation and destruction of money, or to put it another way by *increasing* or *decreasing* the size of the nation's money supply, that the Fed manages its monetary policy.

To see how this works, look at a very simple balance sheet for a Commercial Bank (Figure 8–3). On the left-hand side of the account, traditionally called a T-account because of the T-shape of the dividing lines, are shown the assets of a commercial bank. Assets are simply the holdings of a bank, i.e., the property or money that it holds, owns, or controls. On the right-hand side are the liabilities of the bank, that is, what the bank owes to anyone and everyone.

FIGURE 8-3

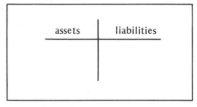

Due to the nature of double entry bookkeeping, with which some readers will be familiar and some not, assets and liabilities must always be equal. That is to say, whatever is held under the control of a bank, or *any* institution for that matter, is automatically owed to someone. Take an example. If you see a corporation that has $1000 worth of cash and buildings on hand, then this $1000 which is of course the assets of a firm, must be *owed* to those people who have lent you the money (perhaps a bank, or bondholders in your corporation) or to those to whom you owe unpaid bills. Any of the $1000 that is not owed in this fashion must automatically represent a claim by the owners, who would be the stockholders if this firm is a corporation. In a sense it can rightly be said that whatever portion of the value of the corporation is NOT owed to outsiders must then be owed to the owners. Thus any sum of assets must at once be represented by an equal sum of liabilities, because what is held or owned by a corporation must be by definition owed to someone, even if that someone is the owner. In short, assets always equal liabilities.

In the case of a commercial bank, by far the largest liability will be what is owed to depositors on account of the funds they have brought in to our bank for safekeeping. If deposits amount to $1000, this $1000 can be shown as a liability.

Our discussion can be simplified enormously if the decision is made to ignore any other kind of liability; which in any case is far more minor in importance.

What can we do with this $1000 if we find ourselves making the bank's policy? One obvious outcome might be the decision to keep the entire $1000 as cash in our vault. (See Figure 8–4.) Here, too, the case will be made easy by ignoring other types of assets which do not help in the understanding of banking, such as the buildings and so forth.

FIGURE 8-4

assets	liabilities
cash in vault $1000	demand deposits $1000

However, if we keep all the deposits we take in as cash in our vault, then fairly soon we will make the horrifying discovery that our bank is not obtaining earnings. There all that money sits; and it will not be too long before one of us is struck with the bright idea that we ought to *lend out* the money in our vaults to suitable borrowers and charge interest. Naturally it will be necessary to keep a sufficient reserve of cash on hand to meet the needs of day-to-day business. It would not do to have to tell depositors that there was not enough in the cash drawer today, so that he couldn't withdraw his funds—maybe next week. However, there will be no need to keep large amounts of cash, due to the fact that except during a banking panic only a small proportion of our depositors will ever wish to withdraw their deposits in a given period of time. That is why Bonnie and Clyde must have found bank robbery disappointing. They would never have been able to find even a very large fraction of a bank's deposits in the vault, because by far the greater proportion had been loaned out to the bank's customers.

MULTIPLE EXPANSION OF BANK DEPOSITS

Now to the crux of the matter. How is it that banks can actually CREATE (or destroy) money? Take a bank (our bank perhaps) into which someone puts $1000 as a demand deposit, that $1000 not having been in the banking system before. For example, it may have lain hidden away in a strong box for many years.

So then what happens? Conducting the analysis in terms of pluses ($1000 has been added to demand deposits) a T-account of the type used earlier will show what takes place. (See Figure 8–5.)

FIGURE 8-5

assets	liabilities
cash in vault +$1000	demand deposits +$1000

Naturally there must be a new liability of the bank, which is the $1000 we owe the depositor. But then the bank has a new asset, the $1000 in soiled old paper notes that the depositor has left in the safekeeping of the bank.

Let us assume that we as bankers feel it necessary to keep only 20% of the cash, called the RESERVE, and will follow the sensible policy of lending out the remaining 80% at interest. (See Figure 8–6.)

What happens to the $800 loan? Presumably it is spent immediately, or it most certainly would not have been borrowed in the first place. Much of the $800 will then find its way back into another bank, or group of banks, as recipients

FIGURE 8-6

assets	liabilities
cash in vault (reserve) +$200 loans +$800	demand deposits +$1,000

of the spending undertaken by the borrower deposit their earnings in their own bank or banks. Any bank into which the loan, when spent, finally gets re-deposited, is called a second generation bank. For simplicity, assume the WHOLE $800 becomes another deposit, as in Figure 8–7, although on a more sophisticated level certain leakages from the banking system would have to be provided for—someone might choose to keep some cash in his wallet, rather than spending it, for example. The whole point of this is that $800 in new money has been created almost out of thin air, because the $800 loan has become a new deposit, and recall that demand deposits ARE money.

FIGURE 8-7

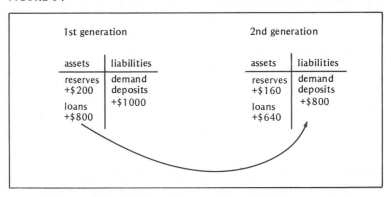

Actually, this can go on and on. If the second-generation banks keep 20% of the deposit in cash as a reserve, they will loan 80% or $640 which will eventually find its way once again back into the banking system as the loan is spent, and recipients of the spending deposit the cash or checks in their own banks, which, following the former logic, are called third generation banks. Thus there is created more new money to the tune of $640.

In turn, 80% of this will be loaned and so on and so on.

There is a simple formula by which one can figure out exactly what the change in deposits is going to be in total, after enough time has passed to allow this process of lending, spending, and re–depositing to work itself out.

That formula is:

$$\text{Final change in deposits} = \begin{array}{c}\text{original}\\\text{new}\\\text{deposit}\end{array} \times \frac{1}{\begin{array}{c}\text{reserve}\\\text{kept (\%)}\end{array}}$$

In the example used here that is $\$1000 \times \dfrac{1}{.20} = \$5000$

This whole process is called the MULTIPLE EXPANSION of bank deposits.

MULTIPLE CONTRACTION OF DEPOSITS

It works in reverse too. Say $1000 is withdrawn from our bank and buried in a tin can so that it never gets back into the banking system. The bank must pay $1000 out of the cash it keeps on hand, i.e., its reserve. Note the T account, Figure 8–8, which shows the bank's total position this time—no pluses or minuses. If it had $10,000 in demand deposits before, keeping $2,000 as a reserve and loaning the $8,000 remaining, it will now find it has only $9,000 in deposits, and—an important fact—cash on reserve is now down to $1000. But that is not 20% of $9000; it is only one-ninth of 11%. So, by not making new loans when old ones are paid off, our bank must reduce its loans to $7,200 and thus hike its reserves to $1,800—or 20% of $9,000.

FIGURE 8-8

(1)		(2)		(3)	
assets	liabilities	assets	liabilities	assets	liabilities
reserves $2000	demand deposits $10,000	reserves $1000	demand deposits $9,000	reserves $1,800	demand deposits $9,000
loans $8000		loans $8000		loans $7,200	

Necessarily the $800 must be pulled out of banks somewhere—second generation banks—for where else do the borrowers lay their hands on the funds to pay off their loans? They get these funds from their bank accounts.

Thus second generation banks lose $800 in deposits. They too will want to cut back their loans to maintain their level of cash–in–reserve at 20% of demand deposits.

In turn, we have demand deposits declining at other banks, the third generation, etc., with the same formula applying as before. This process is termed MULTIPLE CONTRACTION.

This is the means by which money is actually created and destroyed in our banking system. The next chapter will employ this information to see what the federal monetary authorities do to control the creation and destruction to influence the size of the nation's money supply, which is really what monetary policy is.

Questions

1. What are the major ways the equilibrium can be changed through policy decision?
2. When does monetary policy affect investment, and when does it not?
3. What are the various components which make up the money supply?
4. How is the money supply increased? Decreased?
5. What does Multiple Expansion (or Contraction) mean?

9.

MONETARY
POLICY:
Weapons of The Fed

Chapter 8 discussed the important role played by the
commercial banking system in the creation and destruction of
money through alterations in the size of demand deposits,
that is, the ordinary checking account.

This chapter attempts to use this knowledge to see how
monetary policy is made and managed. It will describe how
the Federal Reserve Board, appointed by the President with
headquarters in Washington, makes policy decisions to
manage the enlargement or contraction of the nation's money
supply, utilizing the mechanism for the creation-destruction
of money already studied.

The reason why the Fed would take such action should be
clear by now. To review, an increase in the supply of money
will lower its price, which is the interest rate; a lower interest
rate will have the effect of encouraging more investment.[1]
Finally, an increase in investment means a rise in the C + I + G
schedule, with the expectation that any deflationary gap—
that is, any level of spending lower than that which will
generate full employment—will be eliminated. Naturally the

---

[1]Various hitches in this process, and especially its selective impact, were pointed
out in chapter 8.

mechanism can be put into reverse if an economy has to cope with an *inflationary* gap. Thus total spending C + I + G can be reduced by cutting the money supply, raising interest rates, and thereby discouraging investment.

THE RESERVE REQUIREMENT

The Fed has in its possession three main weapons with which it can influence the supply of money. The first, and a hard-hitting one it is, is the so-called RESERVE REQUIREMENT. In chapter 8 it was noted that bankers will ordinarily, either from custom or prudence, tend to keep a certain percentage of demand deposits in their bank as a reserve; this means that there is a necessity to ensure that the bank will always have sufficient funds on hand to pay off depositors who would like to withdraw their money in the ordinary course of business. But recall also that only a small number of depositors will want to do this in any given day or week, and so the reserve dictated by a banker's own sense of safety can be kept remarkably low—ten percent would be far more than adequate in normal times.

In actual fact, however, both the federal and state governments in this country long ago laid down their *own* rules as to how much has to be kept in reserve. Probably the reason for this is twofold. Making a legal requirement for reserves helps to guard against fly-by-night banking practices. More importantly it allows the authorities to vary the requirements with monetary management in mind.

For banks which are presently members of the Federal Reserve system, there are two categories. Banks located in certain major cities of the US are classified as "reserve city banks," while banks in all other areas of the country are called "country banks." In spite of the rustic name, country banks can be located in very large cities and be powerful financial institutions—it is simply a question of terminology.

According to present law, the reserves which are required to be kept against demand deposits may be set by the Fed within the following range:

For reserve city banks: between 10% and 22%
For country banks: between 7% and 14%

The Fed can change the reserve requirement within those limits, and thereby has a weapon with which it can alter the level of demand deposits. (The weapon is more powerful elsewhere—Sweden can legally go as high as 50%.)

At this point, a moment must be spared to ask where and how these reserves are kept. Up to now, they have been discussed as cash kept in the commercial bank's own vault and ready for duty there. In practice, a high proportion of reserves is *not* kept as cash in the bank's vaults but is instead placed on deposit at the nearest Federal Reserve Bank. All commercial banks which are members of the Federal Reserve System will keep a substantial portion of their reserves on deposit at the Federal Reserve Bank in their district. A map of the districts is shown below. (Figure 9–1.)

FIGURE 9-1
The Federal Reserve System

Source: Board of Governors of the Federal Reserve System *The Federal Reserve System: Purposes and Functions* (Washington, D.C., 1963). p. 16.

Here is even greater reason for budding Bonnies and Clydes to weep; one effect of this is that banks commonly keep far less cash on hand than even their total figure for reserves shows.

RAISING OR LOWERING RESERVE REQUIREMENT

Now back to the use of the reserve requirement as a weapon of monetary management. The Fed's reserve requirement can be *lowered* to fight deflation or *raised* to fight inflation.

Take the CUT first.

For the moment assume that banks are operating under a legal 20% reserve requirement. This is actually larger than presently permitted by law for country banks, but it will simplify the arithmetic a great deal. With the 20% requirement, a balance sheet, or T-account, can be set up for an individual bank which might have the following appearance. (See Figure 9–2.) Note that the bank holds, as demand deposits, $10,000. It is required by law to keep a minimum reserve of $2,000 against these deposits. This means that the bank is free to lend that portion of its deposits which do not have to go into reserve, or $8,000.

FIGURE 9-2

assets	liabilities
reserves $2000	demand deposits $10,000
loans $8000	

Now say the Fed lowers the reserve requirement to 10%. What then will take place? This maneuver means that the bank is obligated to keep only $1000 on reserve against the $10,000 in deposits, freeing an extra $1,000 from reserves and allowing it to be used for lending to customers of the bank. The bank's loans may thus rise to $9,000, and usually we would not expect the bank to pass up opportunities for lending because the bank can earn INTEREST on money loaned (Figure 9–3). If the bank simply chose to let the extra $1,000

FIGURE 9-3

assets	liabilities
reserves $1000	demand deposits $10,000
loans $9000	

sit in its vaults, it would not earn interest. And, not yet mentioned but equally true, even if the bank places the $1,000 in its reserve account at a Federal Reserve Bank, it is no better off because the Fed does not pay interest to commercial banks on these deposits either.

If it is reasonable that the $1,000 will be loaned, then the problem must be faced as to whether the whole process comes to an end here. The answer is no, because it must be assumed that the new $1,000 in loans will be spent by the borrower very quickly, or else he would not have borrowed the money in the first place—he is after all paying for the privilege. If the money is indeed spent it will come into the hands of other businessmen and householders, whose reaction will be to put their receipts in their own bank or banks, which are called as they were before, second generation banks. Once the money is deposited, the banking system will be face-to-face with $1,000 of new deposits. Second generation banks whose combined T-account is shown in Figure 9–4, are legally obligated to keep in reserve $100 but are free to loan the remaining $900 to customers.

As the reader may suspect by now, the process has not ended yet, because the $900 in new loans will eventually come into the hands of recipients, after the money is spent, and these recipients deposit the funds in THEIR banks, which we can term third-generation. And these banks too, after holding 10% in reserve, are free to loan the remainder. And so on and so on, through four, five, and six rounds. The effect then of lowering the reserve requirement is unmistakable. It permits an expansion in the nation's money supply.

Recall what the outcome of this is supposed to be: the money supply increased, which is supposed to make the price of money (interest rate) lower; and this in turn is supposed to persuade businessmen to invest more. In terms of the New Economics, lowering the reserve requirement is an attempt to attack a deflationary gap by raising the $C + I + G$ schedule, hopefully obtaining a new equilibrium at a point

FIGURE 9-4

second generation banks	
assets	liabilities
reserves +$100	demand deposits +$1000
loans +$900	

at or at least closer to noninflationary full employment.

What about the converse? *Raising* the reserve requirement is a weapon against *inflation*. It attempts to lower the money supply, thus raising the price of money for lending (interest rate), discouraging investment and therefore cutting the total spending schedule C + I + G.

If the Fed were to raise the reserve requirement from some starting point, say 10%, the result would be as follows:

On a T-account, demand deposits are $10,000, required reserves are $1,000, an individual bank in this position can loan $9,000.

But if the requirement is raised to 20%, we would find that a bank with $10,000 in demand deposits will now be legally obligated to raise its reserves—remember this is either cash in its vaults or deposits placed by the bank in a Federal Reserve Bank—to the higher figure of $2,000. In order to get the extra $1,000 for its reserves, the bank will somehow have to lower its total lending from the former figure of $9,000 to a new level of $8,000. Readers might jump to the conclusion that the bank calls up borrowers on the telephone and says PAY UP, but of course, even if this were possible it would not be very tactful. What in fact does occur is that the bank will not renew some old loans which come due, nor will they make some new loans which they otherwise could have made with money acquired when old loans are paid off. In this way, the total level of lending is reduced and the bank's reserves built up.

As usual, however, the process does not end at this point; if it did, it would not be of much use for managing the economy. Whoever paid off that $1,000 in loans must have obtained his money from somewhere. Very likely (assume, for now, always) he got it from a demand deposit in a bank. So $1,000 is lost in demand deposits to one or several banks—our old friend, the second generation. This brings the immediate need for second generation banks to build up *their* reserve accounts, because when they paid out the $1,000 it must have come from their reserves.

Second generation banks will reduce their level of lending, resulting in further withdrawals of deposits from third–generation banks, etc. Thus a reduction in the money supply can be achieved.

Changing the reserve requirement is a powerful weapon, and it is actually not used very often. Some examples of its recent use are as follows. During the fairly serious recession of 1958–1960, during the Eisenhower administration and just at the start of the Kennedy era, the reserve requirement for big banks started at a high point of 19½% on Feb. 27, 1958. As the signs of recession deepened, the rate was cut to 19% on March 20, 18½% three weeks later, 18% a week after that, then a delay until Sept. 1, 1960, when it was reduced to 17½%, and finally to 16½% on Dec. 1 of that year. More recently, as a reaction to the present inflationary situation, the reserve requirement was raised to 17%, for reserve city banks, (up from 16½%), and 12½% for country banks (up from 12%) in January, 1968, and again to 17½% and 13% respectively in April, 1969.

However, even though the reserve requirement is a potentially powerful instrument, there is a big problem with it that also applies to the other forms of monetary policy as well. Although it can do a fairly effective job of cutting back the money supply, via restricting loans, it has problems during a depression when the policy is to expand the money supply. The trouble is easy to understand: The Fed can always provide the banking system with plenty of reserves so that banks will be tempted to increase their lending. But the Fed has no legal power to force banks to lend, nor is there any way to compel businessmen to borrow, so that in the depths of a depression, the mechanism for providing excess reserves in the banking system might just not work very well. In any case, banks are likely to be holding more reserves than they are legally obligated to, because reacting conservatively, they fear over-extending themselves.

For at least two more reasons changes in the reserve requirement are not often employed. The first of these is that even small changes in the requirement will automatically lead to sudden changes in banking operations. The weapon cannot easily be graded to give the small adjustments that are needed for effective day-to-day operations of monetary management. For that reason, many bankers and professional economists are not very enthusiastic over changes in the reserve requirement.

Secondly, banks outside the Federal Reserve system —nonmembers—are not subject to the Fed's reserve requirement. This does not mean that they have no legal obligations of this type whatsoever, because nonmembers *will* be subject to the figure for reserves set by the individual states (except for Illinois which has no such requirement). Still it is true that some states usually do not follow the lead of the Fed except after a long time lag, if at all. Hence, especially when the Fed *raises* the reserve requirement it will be penalizing its own members who must constrict their loans, while nonmembers escape scot-free and will be able to lend to the disappointed customers turned away by the member banks.

For these reasons it is perhaps not very surprising that changes in the reserve requirement are generally held back until a major offensive is launched on a wide front against inflation or deflation. In periods which cannot be termed critical, however, this weapon is used infrequently.

THE DISCOUNT RATE

The next form of monetary policy to be taken up is the so-called DISCOUNT RATE, sometimes called the re-discount rate. When the Federal Reserve system was first set up in 1913, (recall that the US was thus one of the last of the great nations to have a government, or central bank) and for many years thereafter, it was expected that the discount rate would be the major means of controlling the size of the nation's money supply. This rate is the interest charged to a member commercial bank which wants to borrow from the Federal Reserve.

If member banks find themselves low on reserves, it is possible for them to borrow funds for their reserve accounts, thus allowing the banks to meet their legal obligations. As might be expected, loans from the Fed to its members ordinarily involve practically no risk, so the rate of interest charged can be kept much lower than rates charged by banks to private borrowers.

The idea is that this discount rate can be manipulated by the Fed over a varying range. For instance, should inflation threaten, the Fed will be expected to raise the discount rate. By this action, borrowing from the Fed is discouraged, and banks which might have been able to avert a contraction in their overall lending by obtaining a loan from the Fed, are not able to do so.

With a low discount rate the opposite is true. Banks are encouraged to borrow, and can avoid contracting their loans— or may even so increase their reserves that they can raise their level of lending. This particular action would, of course, be taken as an anti-depression measure.

There is first the usual objection to all of this. A high rate may very well discourage borrowing from the Fed; that is not denied. But consider a low rate—even one which is fairly near zero. Will this stimulate lending by banks if they find themselves in a very conservative mood due to the depressed condition of the economy? The chances are, that with business poor and prospects dim; banks are simply not interested in extending their current level of lending, and of course there is the concurrent factor at work that businessmen will not be too excited about borrowing during bad times. Thus the discount rate too has its problems during a time of depressed economic activity.

There is another difficulty with the discount rate. In spite of the great importance of this device in many countries and particularly so in Great Britain, where it was developed all through the nineteenth century and still retains a prime position, in the United States it has definitely run up against a psychological barrier. That barrier takes the form that, on the whole, American bankers do not *like* to borrow from the Fed. Many bankers never borrow at all from that source, and in fact there is a well-developed market among commercial banks themselves where any bankers who wish to borrow can find fellow-bankers who wish to lend, thereby avoiding the Fed and its discount rate policies altogether. The reason for this is largely the reluctance of bankers to put themselves in a position of dependence on the Fed; a sort of "we'd rather go our own way" attitude.

This resistance has done a great deal to downgrade the importance of the discount rate in American monetary policy. It usually has a very small actual impact on the size of the nation's money supply.

On the other hand, perhaps *because* its impact is small as far as actual changes in the supply of money are concerned, the discount rate has been used to some extent as a signalling device by the Fed. Should the monetary authorities believe that inflation is in the offing, they can announce, with appropriate fanfare which receives wide coverage by the news media, that the discount rate has been raised. The result will be minute in the way of *direct* influence on the money supply, but it will make clear to anyone possessed of some economic literacy that the Fed is taking a jaundiced view of the threatening inflation and is giving notice that if the situation goes unchanged, it will bring to bear its more powerful weapons. Conversely in time of deflation the discount rate can be lowered as a forerunner or harbinger of further action by the Fed.

In recent years, however, many economists believe that the Fed has been a follower concerning the discount rate rather than a leader, changing it in response to changes in other interest rates instead of as a policy measure. As inflation drives bank interest rates up, the Fed may be forced to raise the discount rate, even if for no other reason than to discourage member banks from borrowing the Fed's funds at the more attractive and relatively lower rate.

Should this be so, the discount rate might have a perverse "announcement effect" in that changes may signal progressing inflation (or vice-versa). Indeed, this same type of adverse effect may apply to reserve requirement changes as well.

Recently there have been some revolutionary new ideas coming out of the Fed in Washington concerning the discount rate, and this chapter will be concluded with a few words about them.

There is a school of thought which argues that the rate at the Fed should be altered much more often (nowadays it does so only about once every year or two). Member banks would be encouraged by the Fed to borrow far more often than they do now. This move seems to be not so much helpful in managing the economy, as perhaps encouraging the smaller banks, now nonmembers of the Fed, to join and make use of the borrowing privileges which are expected to become commonplace under the proposed new discount rate policy. The debate on this within the Fed is a quiet one, and little information is available on when or if the proposals will be adopted. However, as long as inflation remains a serious threat, it is not likely that this reform will be made.

Questions

1. How do changes in the reserve requirement alter the money supply?
2. What is the purpose of discount rate changes?
3. Are there any serious weaknesses in these two forms of monetary policy?

10.

MONETARY POLICY: Weapons of The Fed Continued

This chapter continues the discussion of the weapons available to the Federal Reserve for control of the nation's money supply. A reminder may be in order that the reason such control is desirable is the attack on inflationary or deflationary gaps via manipulating total spending C+ I + G to give an equilibrium level of national income high enough to ensure full employment, but not so high as to be inflationary. Further, monetary policy tries to influence primarily the one element in total spending that may be sensitive to the price of money, that is the interest rate that must be paid for borrowing; and that sensitive element is the level of investment.

In the management of monetary policy it would be very unfortunate if the Federal Reserve system had nothing better to rely on than changes in the reserve requirement and the discount rate discussed in chapter 9. As for the reserve requirement, relying on alterations in it is rather like using a meat cleaver where a stiletto is needed. Moving to the attack with a rise in the reserve requirement when inflation threatens can result in overkill. This policy fails to give fine-tuning, as economists tend to say, and it can be discriminatory against banks which are Federal Reserve members. Fortunately, as is shown a bit later, a stiletto is available.

Changes in the discount rate, on the other hand, though perhaps useful as a signalling device for intended future policy by the Fed, have little to do with actual monetary management so long as member banks are basically unwilling to borrow from the Fed.

OPEN MARKET OPERATIONS

What remains to the Fed? What is the stiletto? The weapon used most often, and the one capable of being adjusted with the utmost delicacy, is known as OPEN MARKET OPERATIONS.

Open market operations, which are directed by the Fed through the medium of a separate committee, comprise the buying and selling on the part of the Fed of United States government securities. These securities are usually short-term bonds; the transactions channelled through about six large private dealers with headquarters in New York City.

To illustrate how open market operations are designed to work, we shall have to use once again an old acquaintance— the balance sheet or T-account for a commercial bank. But this time a second T-account will be employed, this one for the Federal Reserve system itself, because the Fed changes its own holdings via open market operations.

The Federal Reserve system has many items in its assets and liabilities columns, and the Fed's T-account could be complicated a great deal if all were shown. On the other hand, there is good reason to simplify by concentrating on only those assets and liabilities which play a role in open market operations, and that policy is followed in Figure 10–1.

FIGURE 10-1

Federal Reserve System		Member banks	
assets	liabilities	assets	liabilities
US gov't securities	required reserves	required reserves	

An important liability of the Fed is one often discussed without labeling it a liability as yet: the deposits of member banks with the Federal Reserve. Recall that member banks ordinarily will keep a large proportion of their legal required reserves on deposit with a Federal Reserve bank. These reserves make up a fixed proportion of the demand deposits held by any commercial bank. On the right-hand side of Figure 10–1, we see these same required reserves as an asset of member banks.

Meanwhile, of importance on the side of *assets* of the Federal Reserve is one main item: holdings by the Fed of US government securities, which at present represent over $60 billion dollars.

The main lesson of this chapter is that the Fed's decision to BUY or SELL these US government securities will have an effect on the nation's money supply.

Begin with a depression. Here the Fed will want to ensure that the money supply is increased so as to lower interest rates, increase the level of investment, and eliminate the deflationary gap.

The policy it will therefore follow is to BUY US government securities on the open market. The T-accounts for both the Fed and for a single commercial bank, if $1000 in securities is purchased from the general public, will illustrate this. (See Figure 10–2.)

FIGURE 10-2

Federal Reserve System		Commercial Banks	
assets	liabilities	assets	liabilities
① US gov't securities +$1000		③ required reserves +$200	demand deposits +$1000 ②
		④ loans +$800	

First of all, the Fed will end up as proud owner of $1000 worth of bonds or short-term securities that it did not have before. Thus on the asset side of the Fed's T-account, there is a plus figure of $1000. The Fed will ordinarily pay for its newly-purchased securities by writing a check (and for the sake of simplicity, assume that it always does).

The next question is, what happens to the check? Whoever sold the securities to the Fed now has it, and in the normal course of events it will be deposited in the seller's commercial bank, where it becomes a new demand deposit of $1000 which can be seen in the right-hand T-account. Note that this is a new, or net addition to the banking system's sum total of deposits.

The ordinary reaction might be to think that the whole process comes to an end at this point, but by now we should know better. Because, if the legal reserve requirement is 20% (as usual picking a nice round number), then legally the commercial bank in question needs to keep only $200 as reserves, which, as pointed out earlier, are ordinarily kept on deposit at the nearest Federal Reserve Bank. This will allow our bank to seek out higher earnings, which after all is why the bank is in business, by lending out the remaining $800.

As discussed in chapter 9, the lending of $800 to a bank's customers will have further repercussions as the $800 gets spent by the borrowers, and the eventual recipients place the $800 on deposit in their own bank or banks (which we called second generation) as new demand deposits. And as before, the second generation banks which now have $800 in new demand deposits will look at their reserve requirement (20%) and will be strongly tempted to lend to their *own* customers whatever is left over after meeting the figure for reserves. That comes to $160 as the required reserve, with $640 left over for lending. The process goes on and on, until no bank or banks in the system feel any repercussions from the original new deposit of $1000 by the original seller of US government securities to the Fed. We have called this a multiple expansion of demand deposits.

The point is that the Fed can follow the policy of buying securities from the public on the open market whenever it is worried about deflationary conditions in the economy. By doing so it can exert an expansionary influence on the size of the money supply via multiple expansion of bank deposits.

Unfortunately, however, we must again remember that the Fed's open market operations are subject to the same difficulties already discussed with regard to the other types of monetary policy whenever deflation or depression threaten. The Fed can certainly flood the banking system with new deposits, thus providing a large pool of funds which do not have to be kept as reserves (the pool is called excess reserves) and of course there is every reason for the Fed to follow this policy.

Yet no matter how great the level of excess reserves pumped into the system, there is no guarantee that businessmen will want to borrow—they may very well not want to with business conditions looking bad all about them—and at the same time there is no guarantee that banks will want to lend. Ordinarily they would wish to, in order to earn interest; but in bad times, they may prefer to keep excess reserves which they may consider less risky than lending to businessmen when economic conditions are depressed. Naturally they stand to lose the interest they would otherwise earn on their loans, but this may be considered preferable to the much higher losses if businesses begin to fail. In short, banks may be following a policy of safety first, which can tend to upset the effect planned by the Fed when it used open-market operations in the first place.

To gain practice with this concept, turn the whole example around to see what the Fed would do with regard to open market operations if it thought that the country was faced by *inflation*.

In this case the Fed will want to SELL US government securities on the open market. Trace the effect: if the Fed were to sell $1000 in securities to the general public, the T-accounts would show that the Fed's ownership of government securities has declined by $1000 (on the left of Figure 10–3). At the same time, someone will have had to pay the Fed, and we shall assume with good reason that the $1000 in payment comes via a check written by the buyer, a member of the general public, which means that the buyer's demand deposit in some commercial bank will decline by that amount (shown on the right of the figure).

FIGURE 10-3

Federal Reserve System		Commercial Banks	
assets	liabilities	assets	liabilities
① US gov't securities +$1000		③ required reserves −$200	demand depositis −$1000 ②
		④ loans −$800	

If the bank that loses these demand deposits has loaned all that it legally could, again assuming that the reserve requirement is 20%, then it will have kept as a reserve against that $1000 of deposits only $200. It will have to find the extra $800 somewhere, and the usual means of doing so is to reduce the bank's own level of lending by $800. If this occurs, the bank's customers will have to obtain the $800 themselves, and the source of the funds will be second generation banks. Here, in turn, deposits are down, depleting reserves which must be built up to their required level, meaning further contraction in third generation banks, and so forth. The entire process, as we have seen, is called MULTIPLE CON-TRACTION of the money supply.

A short rule of thumb helps to determine the general effect of open market operations. Working in one direction, open market operations may possibly influence the level of demand deposits; working in the other direction they certainly influence that level.

Which is which? When the Fed adds to bank reserves by BUYING securities on the open market, deposit expansion is possible depending on the reaction of commercial banks and their customers who may wish to borrow from the banks.

On the other hand, when the Fed reduces bank reserves by means of SELLING securities on the open market, then deposit contraction is certain as banks are, of course, legally obligated to meet the reserve requirements for demand deposits. Even here though, there may be some delay in the contraction process because banks might be holding on to excess reserves at the time the contraction policy is implemented. If this is so, sales of securities on the open market will have to continue until the whole of these excess reserves are eaten up. Only then will banks find themselves under the necessity of reducing their loans and hence the level of demand deposits in the banking system. Nevertheless, the Fed needs only to continue its selling policy for excess reserves to be eliminated, either sooner or later, so any delays in the effect of the policy would be of a temporary nature only.

Earlier it was seen that open market operations possess some important advantages. Surely the most noteworthy of these is the possibility of extreme smoothness of gradation with very little publicity (and no awkward announcement effects). Open market operations can be used at any conceivable level of intensity from the sale or purchase of a very, very few securities on a day-to-day basis for some careful and gradual fine-tuning adjustment, all the way up to the sale or purchase of a very large quantity which will give a powerful impact. This is by far the most familiar weapon of the Fed.

FEDERAL EXHORTATION

The Fed has a number of less well-known and less important tools that are worth discussing. First on the list is so-called "moral suasion." The word suasion is practically always used by the textbooks on economics, but it means exactly the same thing as the much more familiar word, persuasion. This policy is not very hard to understand. When inflation or deflation threaten, the Fed can use its persuasive powers to see what can be done to avert them. The Fed might be able to use its influence, for instance, to try to control the behavior of member banks as far as their lending policy is concerned. Warnings, exhortations, pleadings, phone calls, telegrams, letters, personal meetings, might all play their role in moral suasion. There is no reason why the Fed should not *try* a policy of this sort, but in truth the experience of history shows that the idea has been substantially a failure. The only exception might be during a period of war or other national crisis when appeals to patriotism can be relied upon. In more normal times, however, moral suasion is not likely to be too much help in combating either inflation or depression unless used in combination with the more orthodox and effective measures of monetary policy.

SELECTIVE CONTROLS

There are also certain "selective controls" as they are known, which can be used when necessary and advisable. In some foreign countries—Great Britain, France, and Sweden are good examples—the use of such controls is a very important adjunct to monetary policy, but in the US we have only a few.

For many years the Fed *had* the power to set limits on private consumer credit, such as that obtained for purchasing a new car or a refrigerator. The Fed was able to set some figure such as a 25% downpayment, five years to pay. Then if inflation threatened and the Fed wanted an additional weapon for control aside from the main forms of monetary policy, it could establish a new regulation such as 75% down, only 1 year to pay. This would, of course, have the effect of lowering the level of consumer demand fairly directly, lowering the C element in C + I + G (that is, aggregate demand) and thereby helping to close the inflationary gap. This selective control was eliminated by Congress in 1952–1953, and it has not been restored even though the Fed argues periodically that it wants it back.

Another form of selective control available to the Fed is the ceiling limitation on interest rates payable on bank deposits.[1] Actually the Fed is free to vary this on savings deposits only—currently it can set a range for member banks between 3% and 6%, and the actual rate is now 4½%. In several foreign countries, including Canada and Great Britain, banks commonly pay interest on regular demand deposits also, and this gives an additional possibility for exerting central bank selective control. But in the US, Congress long ago set the rate at zero for demand deposits.

MARGIN REQUIREMENTS

A third control is the margin requirement. It is well-known that one of the elements which had to do with the onset of the Great Depression of the 1930's was the stock market crash of October, 1929. This great crisis in the stock market, one of the memorable events in American history with its millions in paper profits lost, was a panic that brought about the collapse of business confidence. Its real importance was in influencing businessmen to postpone or cut back their plans for investment; which so reduced aggregate demand that equilibrium national income shifted back substantially. One reason, perhaps the critical one for this crisis in the stock market, was the practice common both then and now of buying on margin. When stock is purchased on margin, the usual sequence sees the buyer paying cash up to a certain percentage of the purchase price, but financing the remainder via a loan from the broker or seller of the stock, using the stock itself

---

[1]That is, savings deposits in commercial banks which are members of the Federal Reserve System.

as collateral or security for the loan. To repeat, buying on margin means borrowing a certain proportion of the stock's price with the stock itself as security for the loan.

There is only one reason why anyone would do things this way—the hope that the price of the stock will rise after it is purchased, eventually allowing the buyer to sell and then pay back the loan. The new, higher price of the stock will mean that the person who bought on margin will be able to repay his loan, and at the same time, realize a tidy sum. Thus buying on margin is part and parcel of stock speculation.

But what happens if, as in 1929, the stock market breaks suddenly and prices decline sharply? In this case it should be evident that the scheme has not worked. If you sell, you take a loss. If you do not sell, you have the loan to repay and must dig into your pocket to find the ready cash. If you have speculated heavily, with a great deal of money borrowed on margin, you may be in too deep to repay the loans; you will have to dump your stock on the market for more or less any price you can get, and the effect will naturally be further declines in the stock market as the enforced selling occurs. The result might then be a deepening crisis of confidence.

The margin requirement was instituted during the depression as a controlling device. A margin requirement of 70% means simply that 70% of the purchase price of stock must be paid for, cash on the barrelhead or by check, while only the remaining 30% can be financed by loans on margin if so desired. If the Fed is concerned about possible adverse effects on business confidence because of speculation in the stock market, it could try to cool the market down by raising the requirement. By law, the legal limit is actually 100%, which would mean a full prohibition of borrowing on margin.

In a recent policy shift, the Fed announced the extension of the margin requirement to apply to loans made by a long list of financial institutions, in addition to the banks and stockbrokers covered originally.

This completes our study of monetary policy: the management of the money supply so as to affect the level of the national product and income. The next chapter turns to fiscal policy: the study of the government's taxation and spending strategy as they apply to the management of the economy.

Appendix

"THE MONETARISTS"

Recent criticisms of monetary policy have been much in the news. Led by Professor Milton Friedman of the University of Chicago, the "Chicago School" of monetarist economics has stirred up a continuing controversy in this area. Friedman believes that the length of time for monetary policy to take effect is a year or more. This lag between implementing a rise or fall in the money supply and the resulting effect on national product is too long, in Friedman's view, to permit the type of monetary policy discussed in the body of this chapter. He believes discretionary monetary policy should be abandoned and replaced by a planned steady growth of from 4% to 5% a year in the supply of money. This view is held by only a minority of economists however.[2]

At this point we may anticipate our discussion of the next three chapters, which considers the spending and taxation policies of government as they influence national product (called "fiscal policy"). Monetarists also hold an unorthodox view in this area. They believe that government spending and taxation take effect on national product primarily through resulting changes in the money supply. Newspapers in recent years have made much of the debate between the monetarists and the more orthodox Keynesian economists, and this controversy is likely to continue for some time.

---

[2]*Friedman's philosophical views also lead him to this conclusion, as he feels political considerations tend to influence the policy decisions of the Fed.*

Questions

1. How do open market operations increase or decrease the money supply?

2. What are the advantages of this form of monetary policy?

3. Why can "buying on margin" give rise to economic problems, and how is this practice controlled?

11.

FISCAL POLICY: Taxation

The last three chapters were concerned with monetary policy
—the means by which the government attempts to control
the economy by regulating the supply of money, in order to
influence the level of investment.

But for every arrow in the quiver of monetary policy, ranging
from the reserve requirement to open market operations,
there is one fundamental objection. The Fed can always
increase or reduce the amount of reserves in the banking
system as much as it wants to, but particularly in a depression
there is no guarantee whatever that banks will lend, or that
businesses will borrow in order to invest. As the Great
Depression showed so vividly, all the exertions of the
monetary authorities may be helpful to be sure, but they
cannot be expected to carry the whole weight of an
assault on depression.

Even during inflation, when monetary policy is expected to
work far more effectively because reserves can always be cut
by the Fed to the point where banks will have to contract
the money supply, there are some problems. One policy which
has been much in the news recently is that fighting inflation
via monetary policy *alone* means raising the interest rate
substantially to choke off investment. But this may affect some

industries and businesses far more than others, and in particular, this is true of the housing market, where interest rates have such great significance for mortgages. In short, interest rates high enough to combat inflation on their own are likely to cause distress to some industries which, from both the standpoint of politics and of fairplay, is perhaps asking a bit too much.

FISCAL POLICY

Thus we turn to the alternative, the child of Keynes and the New Economics, called FISCAL POLICY. Fiscal policy is divided into two parts, one of which is examined here; the other in chapter 12. These two parts are taxation and government spending. Both can affect the level of total spending, or aggregate demand in the economy, and can be used to close inflationary or deflationary gaps when and if they should develop.

An important question is, in what way does taxation or spending policy provide potential management for an economy? Government spending is easy to understand. The government can raise its level of spending and in this way channel new demand into an economy, or lower that level to deflate the economy. However, further discussion of this policy area will be postponed until the next chapter.

TAXATION

We are therefore left with tax policy which works as follows: if taxes are lowered, there will be more income available for households to spend on consumption goods and services, so that obviously, tax reduction can be employed as a weapon against depression—for that is the time when an economy would benefit from raised consumption. It is also hoped that rising consumption will tempt businessmen to invest greater sums than before, reinforcing the expansion. (One difficulty springs to mind. In depression a tax cut may not persuade people to spend as much as they ordinarily would if they feel the prices of the goods they buy are destined to fall. In turn, if business conditions are bad and the outlook for the future dim, there can be no way of guaranteeing that any large increase in investment will take place at all.)

During an *inf*lationary period, the correct tactic would be a *rise* in taxation. The theory is that a greater tax bite will leave less to householders for consumption, and if consumption declines, aggregate spending decreases and the economy is cooled off. This cooling effect will be made stronger if falling consumption leads businessmen to retrench on their investment plans. The major obstacle here must be apparent to every reader. Even though the economist lectures incessantly and churns out articles about the need for a tax increase to halt inflation, he must recognize that taxes are part of politics and that tax increases are very unpopular. The voter who fulminates against them may never realize that they are designed to control the inflation, and thus take less of his income than would be the case if the inflation continued unchecked, eroding his purchasing power. But this reasoning often gets overlooked.

TYPES OF TAXATION

At this point it may be useful to undertake a short discussion of the types of taxation encountered in modern America—a topic clouded with controversy, and in the minds of many economists ripe for further reform. The federal government's tax take is far larger than that of state and local governments, as most readers appreciate when April rolls around and income taxes are due. It is even more important than it seems, however, in that these federal levies are available for alteration as part of the New Economics. (State and local governments can seldom be relied upon to tailor their taxation in the correct direction as part of the battle against inflation and depression.)

FEDERAL

What are the major forms of federal taxation? By far the most important, and representing over half of all federal revenue collected is the personal income tax. Following the reforms of a few years ago, the rate on this tax rises from the lowest figure of 14% to a high of 70% on incomes of $100,000 or over.[1]

Much lower in terms of revenue collected, about a quarter of the total, is the corporate income tax which is now the flat rate of 48% of a corporation's profits. More would be collected here if certain loopholes were blocked up, a notorious one involving the nation's oil companies which are allowed to escape a large chunk of taxation via the oil depletion allowance, write-offs of foreign taxes, and other special advantages.

Ten percent of federal revenues are collected from excise taxes, which are nothing more than a national sales tax on selected goods. Among the rather small list of goods currently subject to an excise tax are gasoline, liquor and beer, wine, cars, tires, long distance telephone calls, airline tickets, cigarettes, pistols, and slot machines—an oddly matched group if there ever was one.

The remainder of federal revenue, approximately 10%, is collected from miscellaneous sources among which the most important are the estate and gift taxes. The estate tax is graduated from 3% to 77% depending on the size of the inheritance left when a person dies; there is a very large $60,000 exemption to this. It is obviously necessary to have a gift tax too, as people would be able to escape the levies on inheritance by giving away property before death. This tax is lower in percentage terms, ranging from about 2% to 58%, but it also has a much lower exemption, only $3,000. Several loopholes mean that few people ever pay the maximum rate. Western European countries such as Great Britain are much stricter on this score. As noted before, any or all of these taxes are variable as part of the government's fiscal policy, if enough votes can be garnered in Congress to change the law.

STATE

Briefly we can survey the other forms of taxation in the US. The state governments depend chiefly on the sales tax, which ranges from a high of 6% in Alabama and Pennsylvania, down

---

[1]*Because it rises as a percentage of income, it is called a "graduated" tax.*

to zero in a few states such as New Hampshire. A much smaller but rising source of tax revenue is the state income tax, sometimes a flat rate such as 2% of all income, sometimes a graduated rate so that the rich pay proportionately more than the poor. Currently, the highest rate levied by states is in New York and New Jersey where very high incomes are subject to a 14% tax. Economists are usually far more in favor of the income tax than the sales tax, first because the former can be graduated according to ability to pay whereas the latter will bear with proportionately greater weight on lower income groups, and second because income tax receipts grow faster than do sales tax receipts as incomes rise. The first state income tax, by the way, was a temporary Massachusetts levy imposed in the 1630's when Harvard University was being founded (more accurately it would have to be called a provincial tax).

LOCAL

Local governments, on the other hand, depend traditionally on the property tax. Here too, economists will have to point out that the property tax is inferior to the income tax on the score of fairness, because one person who uses his income for a nice house and land will be heavily taxed whereas his neighbor who chooses a modest home but extended vacations in Bermuda and nights in fancy clubs will pay far less to the local government. Furthermore, land is often taxed on its most profitable use, so that orchards and farmlands are sold to housing developers or for commercial buildings. Some local governments are now instituting a sales tax—New York City is a familiar example. But major attention has been focused in recent years on the local government INCOME tax.

This is not all that modern actually. Philadelphia had one as early as 1938; by 1968 over one hundred and seventy cities had them. They are usually flat rate; but are occasionally graduated as in New York City and Baltimore. Nowadays the local income tax is found in small cities scattered all across the country, in places like Paducah, Kentucky, and Gadsden, Alabama; it can represent the most important form of local government revenue as in Columbus, Ohio, where over 70% of the municipality's funds come from this source.

The major criticism of the local income tax is that it is usually

NOT graduated, unlike the situation in New York and Baltimore, and that it is levied for the most part on only certain forms of income, such as wages and salaries, while dividends or capital gains[2] are not taxed at all. Thus, the situation is often a discriminatory one, loaded against the wage-earner.

A DECADE OF TAXATION POLICY

From this point we shall be examining the use of taxation in the US during the past decade, asking in particular how have tax changes been used to control the nation's economy? During this discussion do not forget that it is usually ONLY the federal government's taxation which is altered to control the economy; state and local governments seldom have the skill, the inclination, or the unity of purpose to manage their own fiscal policy.

During the years of the Eisenhower administration, when men like George Humphrey and Robert Anderson were Secretaries of the Treasury and Maurice Stans (now Secretary of Commerce) was at the Bureau of the Budget, there was an easily identified antipathy toward the New Economics in Washington. Three serious recessions[3] in American economic history occurred during the Eisenhower administration—in 1953–1954, 1957–1958, and again in 1960 and the beginning of 1961. During this period the failure to use the tools of Keynesian economics was, if not disastrous, at least extremely costly in terms of output lost from the recessions, and the human waste of widespread unemployment (which hit the highest levels during these years, nearly 8% in 1958, since before World War II). It is estimated that the US was losing, on a yearly basis, from $25 to $30 billion worth of output, that is, national product, during these times.[4] The sheer size of this figure ought to stimulate quite a bit of thought: for one thing, not including battle deaths and injuries, that would add

---

2If 10 shares of stock or an acre of land are purchased in 1971 for $600 and sold in 1972 for $1000, that represents a "capital gain" of $400. Even the federal government taxes capital gains less heavily than income, which is a controversial point.
3A "recession" is a milder form of a depression.
4Output that would have been produced had the unemployed men, land, machines, etc., been at work.

up in total to considerably more than the Vietnam war has cost us annually.

After the inauguration of John F. Kennedy in 1961, a new wave of economic thought swept over Washington. Mr. Walter Heller was one of the most instrumental figures in this wind of change. The idea has already been explored several times that a lowering of taxes will release income for expanded consumption spending by households, generating greater investment by businesses, thus raising the schedule for total spending and moving to eliminate the economy's deflationary gap.

The Kennedy administration soon adopted this theory and passed the first major tax reduction in American history which was strictly designed as a measure of New Economics fiscal policy: this was the so-called investment tax credit which allowed businesses to reduce the tax they had to pay by a certain percentage (7%) of the investment they had undertaken during the year. This was the first use of a type of tax much in the news in 1971, as we shall see.

Though the investment tax credit helped, it was really not strong enough to do the trick entirely. In the period 1962 to 1963 the economy was still not performing to capacity. Keynesian economists suggested a more general cut in tax rates was necessary in order to generate a full-employment, full-output situation, and early in 1963 the Kennedy administration proposed a major decrease in taxes.

The process of getting these tax cuts through Congress was long and painful and it was not until February of 1964, with Lyndon Johnson as president, that the so-called Revenue Act of 1964 was passed. Under its terms, personal income tax rates were cut all across the board by about one quarter. Meanwhile, the corporation tax was reduced from the old figure of 52% of profits to 48%. At the time of the bill's passage, it represented a total reduction in the tax bill of about $13 billion; in 1967, with a higher national income and higher prices, the figure was $18 billion less than it would have been at the old rates.

Naturally, when the government reduces taxes without any commitment to reduce spending, there is a tendency to cause a deficit in the budget. Because of this, some observers spoke of runaway inflation, national bankruptcy, Robin Hoods of the Red Ink, and other equally witty phrases.

The truth, however, is that this measure of Keynesian fiscal policy was amazingly successful. By the first half of 1965, with new spending percolating through the system as consumption and investment were both raised, the gap between actual GNP and the potential figure which could have been reached at full employment, had narrowed, according to the *Federal Reserve Bulletin*, "by more than one-half from the 25 billion to 30 billion dollar gap that had prevailed earlier. . . ."[5]

To continue from the *Bulletin*, "Even so, there was still some concern in early 1965 about the tendency for actual GNP to fall short of its potential. To help offset this continuing fiscal drag, and at the same time make good on a long-deferred promise to reduce . . . taxes levied in World War Two, a . . . cut in Federal excise taxes was enacted in the spring of 1965." This covered areas such as automobiles, long distance telephone calls, and so forth, and reduced the tax burden by about $2 billion in the year following June, 1965.

The progress that the economy made in 1965 was a vindication of the New Economics. In that year gross national product had increased by 6% in real terms in comparison with the very poor 2½% in, for example, 1959 to 1960. Prices rose by less then 3%. At the same time in 1965, unemployment was reduced by a full percentage point from the 1962–1963 average and more than 2 percent from the 1958 figure. All this, note, without the stimulus of increased spending in Vietnam. One reason this data is so illustrative is that escalation in Vietnam had not yet come about—and thus in a classic textbook sense, which may well be remembered by economic historians for a very long time, the New Economics showed it could work to increase national product.

Then, of course, the waters became muddied by the vast increase in US involvement in Vietnam. Defense expenditures by the government mounted rapidly. The chief period of activity was from the first quarter of 1965 to the middle of 1966, when commitments (that is, contracts and other obligations incurred on a yearly basis) rose from $50 billion to over $75 billion. Other government expenditures rose as well, though they were not nearly as important in total as defense. Particularly significant increases in spending went for

---

[5]*This and the following quotations are from "Federal Fiscal Policy in the 1960's," Federal Reserve Bulletin, Sept., 1968, pp. 701–718.*

educational grants to public schools and colleges, and social security including medicare.

Because of Vietnam, the New Economics had to shift its stance toward lowering total spending instead of increasing it. And here again Keynesian fiscal policy was resorted to as a measure of economic control. Early in 1966 the first comments began to be heard that a tax increase would be necessary to keep the economy from overheating, and serious inflation from developing.

In fact, prices had already started to rise as the impact of higher spending was felt. For example, if, on average, one dollar's worth of goods and services in 1958 were purchased in 1964, it would still have cost only $1.08. But with Vietnam and other spending, the same amount of goods would have cost $1.13 in 1966, $1.16 in 1967, and about $1.20 in the first half of 1968. As pointed out earlier, monetary policy was used to try to control this, but the raising of interest rates had to be pushed so far that, according to the Fed, "these pressures were creating signs of disorder in financial markets . . ." such as housing.

President Johnson requested a temporary tax increase in early 1967—a 6% surcharge or addition to the tax bill—on both personal and corporate income taxes. Congress procrastinated for a very long time, nor can it really be said that President Johnson supported the proposal with much enthusiasm. This, in spite of the fact that most economists had been arguing for a tax increase since the year before, 1966. With inflation continuing, action was delayed so long that the administration was forced to ask for a greater surcharge, 10% of the tax bill. The 10% surcharge was passed in June, 1968, as part of the Revenue and Expenditure Control Act of 1968. As the name of the act shows, government spending was included in its provisions, but discussion of that will be delayed until the next chapter.

The thing to note is that once again fiscal policy took a long time to implement. From the time the need was felt in 1966 to the actual passage of the increase was about two years. This is really much too long. Even in the best of circumstances time is a factor. It takes time for a need to be recognized, and then for the proper fiscal policy to be drawn up. After the whole thing has been passed there is the additional time needed for the tax to have an impact on the economy.

But in the US, using tax increases and cuts as fiscal policy runs afoul of the Congressional prerogative to pass tax legislation. Every time Keynesian fiscal policy is used, some Congressmen will delay a tax bill on the grounds that higher taxes are bad, period. They send a chill down the backbone of every voter, and thus vicariously down the legislator's backbone. This so often happens even though the economist will point out that the taxpayer will lose more, and probably far more, if taxes are kept the same but inflation is allowed to erode the purchasing power of the dollar. Other Congressmen, better informed this time, will attempt to block a tax bill on the grounds that there are so many loopholes that reform is necessary. The big oil company that benefits from the depletion allowance, the taxation of capital gains at a rate less than income, no taxes on municipal bonds, etc., are things that trouble many thoughtful people. But sometimes it must be recognized that the control of inflation must be speedy, whereas reform has got to be, from its controversial nature, a slow process. In fact, the last three years have shown quite forcefully that the delay in passing the tax cut was disastrous for the control of inflation. Once businessmen, labor unions, and consumers had become accustomed to rates of inflation of 4, 5, or 6%, as was true by 1968, then the inflationary spiral became much more difficult to break. When unions are convinced that prices will rise, they press hard for wage increases; similarly businessmen will build regular increases into their price structure. What this amounts to is another classic case—a case of "too little, too late" as far as the tax increase of 1968 is concerned.

Another problem with tax changes, perhaps even more important, is that they take far too little account of pressing social issues. For one thing, if taxes are reduced to fight a deflationary situation this will increase private spending all right, but it will only do so among that class of people who pay taxes in the first place. The poor who do not pay any income tax will receive no direct benefit.[6] Furthermore, tax reductions which release funds to the private sector may be welcome to most everybody, but they tend to ignore in part the pressing needs for various social types of spending. Think

---

[6]Although the expected improvement in the economy should expand employment opportunities for the poor.

of areas where more federal spending is essential: slums and the ghetto, primary, secondary, and university education, medical care for the elderly and indigent, as well as for the working man, who more and more often faces appallingly high medical bills as the cost of medical care has sped ahead faster than any other category listed in the consumer price index. Highways, urban transportation, conservation including parks and scenic areas, control of water and air pollution, all fall into the category of problems which are *unlikely to be righted* without the use of federal money.

SUMMARY

It is apparent that tax *decreases* can generally get passed, though even this in 1964 was at tortoise rather than hare speed. Tax *increases*, however, run up against the obvious road block of reticence to pay higher taxes no matter what the purpose. Countries like Canada, Great Britain, and Sweden do not have this problem to any great degree because of their parliamentary system of government which speeds the passage of major legislation. Other countries such as West Germany which are federal in nature have special laws which allow the government to alter taxes within certain limits without having to get a bill through the legislature. This has been talked about in this country, but is at present far from being adopted. Thus, to a large extent, Keynesian fiscal policy in the tax area is shackled.

Questions

1. What is "fiscal policy"?
2. Why are federal taxes more important than state and local taxes in controlling the economy?
3. Why is it said of taxes that it is harder to attack inflations with them than it is to attack depressions?

12.

FISCAL POLICY: Spending

The other important area of fiscal policy is the government's *own* spending, including not only federal but also state and local government spending.

This very large figure is, it should be clear, available for manipulation if the policies of the New Economics are understood. The principle is straightforward. If total spending, or aggregate demand, is C + I + G, then the government can increase that schedule by increasing its own spending (as in Figure 12–1). It can also push it back by the simple act of

FIGURE 12-1

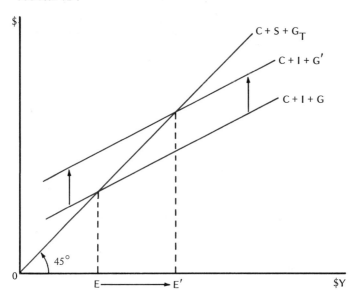

cutting its total spending. In either case, the equilibrium level of national income can be shoved *upward* or *downward* in order to eliminate any deflationary or inflationary gap as it develops.

What exactly is federal spending nowadays? The fiscal 1970 figures made up a grand total of 197 billion dollars.[1] (A little bit of a shock, by the way, considering that the entire total of spending by the US government from 1789 to 1849 was only about one billion dollars, and from 1850 to 1899 only about $15 billion. Even as late as the 1920's, the government was spending only about $3 billion per year.)

What about that $197 billion total? The first surprising fact is how much of it is connected with defense or past wars. The biggest single item (see Table 12–2) is national defense at about 42% of the budget. About $20 billion of that was devoted to the war in Vietnam. But considerably more is actually devoted to wars, in this case *past* wars, as for example, the second item in the table, veteran's benefits. The higher total for interest on the national debt might not seem to have much connection with military activity, but it certainly does. In 1940, the national debt was about $48 billion. By 1946, with World War II just over, that debt had grown to $270 billion. Twenty-four years later at the beginning of 1970, the debt stood at not much higher than this: $368 billion. Whether or not readers of this book think a big national debt is something to lose sleep over; whether or not it is a sin, a disgrace, or a danger, it will most certainly have to be agreed that, based on the statistics just quoted, by FAR the greater amount of the debt was incurred to fight World War II, and thus most of the interest now paid yearly on the debt is in itself payment for a war long over.

Aside from this, the table shows the other major forms of spending by the federal government: international affairs, including foreign aid; health, education, and welfare; agriculture and natural resources; commerce, housing, and transport; the space program; and lastly, a miscellaneous category.

In addition to all this there is the spending of state and local governments: state government spending in recent years has been about $60 billion annually, with the only large

---

[1] *Including outpayments for the social security program.*

items for states the very familiar ones, highways and education. For local government, spending is a little higher than $60 billion, and this time there is only one very large item— education. One point concerning these is the same with state and local taxes—they are not likely to be altered as part of Keynesian economic policy.

TABLE 12–2

US Government Budget
Outlays, Fiscal Year 1970
(June 1970—June 1971)

	In billions of dollars	% of total rounded off
Total	196.6	100
National Defense	80.3	41
(Vietnam: about 20%)		
Veteran's Benefits	8.7	4
Interest on National Debt	18.3	9
International Affairs	3.6	2
Health, Education, Welfare	64.1	33
Agriculture, Natural		
Resources	8.7	4
Commerce, Housing, Transport	12.3	6
Space Program	3.7	2
Miscellaneous*	−3.0	−1

The minus sign is due to a budgeting technicality covering interest receipts and pension fund contributions which need not concern us here.

GOVERNMENT SPENDING: TRANSFERS AND PUBLIC WORKS

Basically, there are two types of policy that are most often used if the attempt is made to manage the economy by changing government spending. The first is by altering the level of payments to individuals and groups; this can include a fairly large number of items such as transfers (veteran's benefits, changes in social security payments, additions to state unemployment benefits) or increases in government employment via grants to school districts, urban renewal authorities, and so forth. The second method is labelled public works projects.

Some comments on the usefulness of changing the level of payments to individuals and groups may be made. In time of depression this will naturally have the effect of increasing total spending: the only possible interference might be that some of the new income will be saved; but on the other hand, the poorer the economy the less likely this will be.

Probably the major problem with this form of fiscal action is the fairly obvious tendency for grants of this sort to become permanent. Once pressure groups such as veteran's organizations, associations of welfare recipients, or the elderly who receive social security become accustomed to a certain level of payments from the government, then it will be politically (and morally) very difficult to cut back these payments as a measure of fiscal policy.

If a president and congress want to protect their position, the only direction which can be traveled is UP in this type of grant. Just imagine for a moment the outcry that would occur, and no doubt rightly so, if the government were to attempt to cut back on social security or veteran's benefits during inflation.

The problem is essentially the same for other forms of government spending when the attempt is made to cut back as an antiinflation move. The question is always WHERE? As congress and the president found in 1968 when trying to make the 6 billion dollar cut in spending that went along with the tax increase, and as President Nixon found in the trimming operations of 1969, 1970, and 1971, it is not easy to find the places to make the cuts. Only half in jest, it seems that the federal budget is divided into three categories: those sorts of spending that could easily be reduced for the welfare of the country but cannot be due to the very strong political support they receive; those which are a fairly ironclad legal obligation; and those which can be cut rather easily because they do not have powerful voting blocks behind them, but are very important to a healthy country with a growing population.

Take some examples. The author finds it easy to pick on some federal spending, past or present, that he believes to be of marginal benefit and which would probably not be in the budget except for the very strong congressional support they receive. Examples include obsolete navy, air, and army bases kept in service long after they should have closed; the super-expensive Supersonic Transport (SST) and other aid for the aircraft industry. No doubt readers could keep naming pet examples of their own. But congressmen fight for these projects—they bring industry to a state; the congressman gets his name in the headlines, voters remember him at the next election. It is all a very old story, compounded by the fact that to oppose spending on the nation's defense is equated in the minds of some people with being less than patriotic. Then take the government's payments to farmers to keep their incomes up. The farm bloc in congress is big enough to achieve this, in spite of very persuasive arguments that the aims of the agricultural price-support program should be thoroughly re-evaluated. These are just some of the areas where political power allows programs to continue unchanged, and so the logically cuttable is not cut.

However, some forms of spending are, as stated earlier, legal obligations. Interest on the national debt, payments to veterans, and social security are all examples.

What then *is* open to possible reduction? The list includes all those categories which have made this country a land of social tension in the past few years. Education, health programs such as medicare and medicaid, welfare, natural resources, commerce, housing, transportation, and finishing up with those often-attacked orphan-stepchildren, foreign aid and the space program. In every one of these areas there are established programs of great national importance, either in the sense of actual physical attainment or in establishing a social climate. Yet all of them tend to be more "cuttable" than the programs supported by the big voting blocs, or those which are statutory obligations.

So, in short, raising government spending as a weapon against depression works well, but the fiscal policy of cutting spending to fight inflation does not tend to work as well.

PUBLIC WORKS

Now consider public works spending: the idea being, of course, that the federal authorities can institute a program of public works spending as a weapon against depression, and hold down such projects when inflation threatens.

There is no question that public works can pump an almost unlimited amount of spending into the economy, and this was one of the great accomplishments of the Roosevelt era. Federal highways and farm-to-market roads, rural electrification, dams for power and flood control including the huge Tennessee Valley Authority, public parks, sidewalks, airports, and an almost endless variety of other schemes. Through the agency of the Works Projects Administration (WPA) and the Civilian Construction Corps (CCC) among others, this weapon against depression was widely used, in the 1930's.

There is, however, a significant problem with public works projects that cannot be ignored. First, the economic need has to be recognized. Then, while financing is obtained from congress, it will be necessary to formulate plans which may be extensive, draw up blueprints and cover all other vital details, and then labor will be hired, managerial skills acquired somewhere, and land obtained. Land might involve the government in lengthy condemnation proceedings which may add to an already long time lag. And, if the planners are unlucky, it could mean that the new spending starts to pour out into the economy just about the time the depression has been cured by other means. Then the spending will have to be treated as too stimulating, and worst of all it might actually have the effect of generating an inflation.

With this in mind, it must be recognized that public works projects, however useful to an economy they are, form an imperfect tool of fiscal management in the American economy.[2]

An economist soon comes to admire certain European countries which have gone a long way toward handling this difficulty with public works. Many years ago Sweden instituted a so-called shelf of public works projects, planned and ready-to-go on just a few months' notice. Then when depression threatens, the government can turn to the shelf and implement those programs which it considers have the highest priority. The idea is spreading. West Germany, in 1967, adopted something of the same thing; and it is difficult not to be impressed by these plans. Public works are going to be used as an anti-depression device in any case, so the more constructive thought that has been directed to the question

---

[2]Though the text concentrates on mechanical objections to public works programs, there are some philosophical objections too. In particular, people who believe that "big government" is disadvantageous will prefer tax cuts to public works. They will argue that the growth of government spending (federal, state and local) as a percentage of GNP is far too high, having moved from 18% in 1940 to 21% in 1950, 27% in 1960, and 32% in 1970.

"Where can the spending be used to do the most good for the economy?" the better off a country would seem to be.[3]

It has to be noted that public works are still not politically popular as a policy measure in some quarters, especially among those who feel the federal budget should always be balanced. It must be made clear that if the government launches new programs to increase total spending in the economy, it will certainly not want to raise taxes to cover that spending. If it DID, then the new spending would simply be offset by the new taxation. What the government adds to the economy with one hand it would be subtracting with the other.[4] Note, however, that when the government spends more than it takes in as taxation, that is a budget *deficit*, and right there we get into politics. Back in 1958, when the US was right in the middle of the sharpest recession since World War II, with unemployment rising and total output falling, President Eisenhower refused to turn to public works (or tax cuts for that matter). As Mr. Eisenhower said, he was opposed to "going too far with trying to fool with the economy."

This led Democrats in Congress (that party controlled both House and Senate in 1958) to propose their own anti-recession measures, led by the then Senate Majority Leader, Lyndon Johnson. A bill passed the House and Senate in March for the speeding up of construction projects for which money was already appropriated.

Again in March, an emergency highway bill was passed which expanded spending on the road system by a very large amount. (This became the Interstate Highway Program which therefore did not germinate in the Kennedy administration as many people tend to assume, but in the Eisenhower period.) Even though he signed the bill President Eisenhower did not

---

[3]In June, 1971, Mr. Nixon vetoed a $5 billion emergency public-works bill passed by Congress on the ground that its impact on unemployment would take far too long to be realized, and the veto was sustained by Congress in July.
[4]More advanced books show that $1 in new government spending is not exactly counteracted by $1 in new taxes. The principle is called the "Balanced Budget Multiplier," and works this way: $1 in new government spending will pump out into the economy just that: $1. But $1 in new taxes will reduce spending by less than $1 because not all of a person's income is spent for consumption. Some of it is saved. Spending may go down by only 95¢, and saving by 5¢, when $1 worth of new taxes are levied. To repeat, then, new government spending stimulates the economy slightly more than an equivalent amount of taxation cools it off.

think too highly of the emergency highway measure; he viewed it with "serious misgivings."

Finally, an omnibus river, harbor, and flood control bill was passed. This was too much of the New Economics for Mr. Eisenhower, and he vetoed it. After many changes he finally signed a substitute bill in July. The point of all this is simply to point out that political opinions may present a distinct obstacle to the use of federal public works projects.

A last difficulty is an argument that was often heard in the heady days of the New Deal. It is possible that government public works may compete with and reduce the level of *private investment*. It is certainly not out of the question that this could occur, but if it should, it would mean that the federal authorities had not done their homework very well! Surely it would not be terribly difficult to dream up projects that are not in competition with the private sphere; and although there may be a problem here, it seems far from insoluble.

FINANCING A FEDERAL DEFICIT

Thus fiscal policy involves BOTH changes in the level of taxation and in the level of government spending. If, as a cure for depression, the government must tax less, or spend more, or both, then the national budget will go into deficit. Readers may have asked themselves, where does the money come from if you want to spend more than you take in?

Actually there are a number of ways in which this could be done. Many governments, including ours at certain times in history, have financed a deficit (that is, found the means of providing the government with money to spend over and above what it collects in taxes) by simply running the printing presses. Just send a messenger over to the printing office and tell them to run off $50 billion worth of dollar bills and have them ready by tomorrow morning. That will give the government the means to raise its spending, and if the country is in a depression, that is in fact what is needed—to raise spending. However, this method is now outdated. The same effect can be achieved by more sophisticated means that are not as crude as running the presses. In any case, printing new money has traditionally been associated with wild inflations, such as those which occurred in Germany, the Confederate States, and the Thirteen Colonies. These governments kept printing money long after full employment had already been reached, so prices had to rise. There is no reason why the technique could not be used if the authorities have the will power to stop the presses when full employment is reached—but in any case, it is politically unpopular and not usually done.

Another way to spend more than is currently being taken in via taxes, is by raising tax rates. Readers should see that this will not help the economy. If more is spent, fine, but if taxes are increased to pay for it, then consumption will certainly decline. So all that has been done is to raise spending with one hand and restrict it with the other.[5]

Another alternative, perhaps, is to borrow funds from the public by selling bonds to them. This would be fine if people buy bonds with money which has been sitting in banks at a time when banks are not lending and businesses do not want to borrow because of a depression. On the other hand, there is the possibility that government sales of bonds will only siphon funds away from alternative uses such as consumption and investment. If such a diversion takes place then the increase in government spending financed by the bonds will just balance the decreased consumption and investment, which will not do any good at all.

Fortunately, there are two other ways for the authorities to get all the money they need without diverting funds from other forms of spending and without having to risk political disaster by turning out printing press currency. In a depression banks probably will be keeping large amounts of funds which they have neither the opportunity nor the inclination to lend out on advantageous terms. We have called this *excess reserves* in the banking system. The government will thus probably be able to sell bonds to the banking system, because these bonds are perfectly safe (though using the word "perfectly" is a bit exaggerated for those who bought Imperial Russian bonds in 1914 or Third Reich bonds in 1938). Nevertheless, banks will prefer to earn interest on government securities, and the authorities end up with additional spending power. This can

---

[5]Remember, however, that for strict accuracy the theory of the Balanced Budget Multiplier has to be considered, for which see footnote 4, p. 132.

be continued as long as necessary if excess reserves are pumped into the banking system by the Fed; the process is fairly painless, and will not ordinarily constrict either consumption or investment.

Even so, we are forced to admit that under some terribly adverse circumstances it is possible that the government will not be able to sell its bonds to commercial banks. There is a way out of this dilemma. If necessary, the authorities may borrow from the Federal Reserve System. There is a very neat trick here. The Fed is sold, for example, $1,000 in US bonds. In return, it compensates the government by giving the US Treasury a $1,000 checking account in some Federal Reserve Bank, which can be spent as any other checking account. In practice, there is no reason why an unlimited amount of money could not be made available for anti-depression spending via this route; and it does not take much perception to see that this is really exactly the same thing as running new ten-dollar bills off the printing presses—because either way new money is created. (Remember that checking accounts, or demand deposits are money just as much as coins or paper bills.)[6] So, to conclude, the government need never be starved for money to spend if it wants to spend more than it taxes—that is, run a deficit.

Now for fighting INFLATION, the weapon is to run a surplus by taxing more than spending. This can be achieved by the dual process of reducing federal spending, or raising taxes, or both. This is going to result in a budget surplus. What should be done with the surplus of funds collected if Washington decides to use this sort of fiscal policy? We know enough by now to say that it cannot be spent, for if it is spent, the anti-inflationary impact is lost.

On the other hand, part of the national debt could be paid off with the surplus, but this too is somewhat self-defeating. This is because as the debt is paid off, that is as people get paid money for the US government bonds they hold, these same people will turn around and spend some part of their receipts, which is certain to reduce the antiinflationary effect.

Another solution might be for the government to take the surplus cash and simply burn it. But as economist Campbell

---

[6]*This method was last used on any scale during World War II.*

McConnell says, this would be considered an "act of considerable obscenity" because voters would not tend to understand the reasons for this destruction.

Again, however, there is a more reasonable way to act. The surplus can be added to the idle bank accounts of the Treasury, insulated from the rest of the economy so that they will not be loaned out. This could easily be accomplished if the Treasury keeps the surplus deposited with a Federal Reserve Bank, where it cannot be touched by private borrowers in the economy.

THE BUILT-IN STABILIZERS

One last topic will end our look at basic fiscal policy. The last two chapters discussed changes in taxes, and alterations in government spending, which, when pushed through congress, can be used to eliminate inflationary or deflationary gaps. But in addition to these actions, called discretionary fiscal policy, it has long been recognized that due to the way our economy is organized, fiscal policy also tends to work *automatically* to some degree at least. The idea is simple enough. When a period of deflation is entered, incomes go down. Our tax system collects a certain percentage of income, and therefore in an economic slump, tax receipts are reduced. Note that this lower taxation is exactly what is required to fight depression. Naturally it works in the opposite direction: higher national incomes mean more collected in taxation, which is just the dampening effect that is wanted when inflation threatens.

Automatic action can also be seen in some forms of government spending. During depression, relief and other unemployment benefits rise in step; with inflation, far less is paid out on this account, without anyone passing any new laws. Agricultural price supports have an identical effect, with more paid out in depression, less in inflation, which is again just what Dr. Keynes ordered. All these are called the "built-in stabilizers." With taxes alone, the US Commission on Money and Credit stated that as much as 33 to 40% of the rises or falls in national income is offset by the built-in stabilizers.

Questions

1. How do changes in federal spending play a role in Keynesian fiscal policy?
2. What are the disadvantages of public works projects as an instrument of fiscal policy? How might these disadvantages be overcome?
3. How can government acquire the money to finance a deficit for the purposes of fiscal policy?
4. What are "built-in stabilizers" and what do they do?

13.

A POSSIBLE DETERRENT TO FISCAL POLICY: The National Debt

In chapter 12, it was suggested that a balanced budget, where government taxation is equal to government spending, is not always the correct economic policy to employ. Even worse, balancing the federal budget may have the totally unwanted effect of deepening depressions and heating up inflations. Here this problem of a balanced budget is taken up in detail.

For centuries many politicians have treated it almost as a fetish. As educated ancient Romans paid lip service to Jupiter and the other gods even though they did not for a moment believe in all that rigamarole, so do many statesmen feel the necessity of supporting a balanced budget in spite of the fact that an enormous majority of professional economists stand ready at the drop of a statistical abstract to show that always balancing the budget is misguided, counter-productive, and in terms of the economic misery generated, politically disastrous.

Even President Nixon, in the 1968 campaign, felt it necessary to say that he would balance the budget to cure inflation. The point is that important people keep using the term and get cheered for it—as during Mr. Nixon's campaign. More recently, some of the emergency measures of August 1971, clearly reflected the ethos of budget balancing.

BALANCED BUDGETS

There have been so many arguments in favor of a balanced budget that it is difficult to know where to begin. Families must earn as much as they spend, it is said, or bankruptcy will threaten—the same must be true of the national government.

Then too, if government runs large deficits, this will increase the NATIONAL DEBT, and if that gets too high, the US will be in deep trouble. And so on.

First of all we will attempt to show that, in the language of Keynesian economics, a balanced budget can make a depression or an inflation worse. Assume that the government always balances its budget, which is not too far from the expressed desires of President Eisenhower and a number of his advisors in the 1950's. Then say that for some reason, total spending begins to sink to a low level, a level so low that national income will not be high enough to generate full employment (as in Figure 13–1, which shows C + I + G and the 45° line). Here equilibrium income is below that which gives full employment.

If income does sink in this fashion, what will happen to the federal budget? Before income declined, tax collections were

FIGURE 13-1

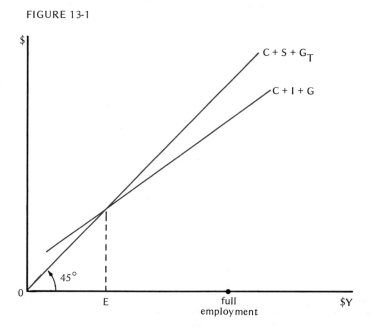

equal to spending, or Gt = G (a balanced budget in other words). Does anything happen automatically as national income sinks? Recall our discussion of built-in stabilizers in chapter 12: as the most important taxes are expressed as a percentage of national income, less income means less collected in tax revenue, or Gt down. And what about spending? In depression, unemployment benefits, the farm support program, and so forth, automatically pour more money into the economy. Without any conscious effort whatever, the budget goes out of balance and the nation finds itself in deficit (this is what happened to President Eisenhower in the late 1950's when a recession hit the country, and to President Nixon in 1970–1971, during which fiscal year the deficit was over $20 billion).

If the authorities feel compelled to pursue a balanced budget, what then will they do? They will have to raise taxes, or cut government spending, or both, until equality in taxes and spending is again achieved. Note, however, what this does to our Keynesian diagram (see 13–2). The reduction in government spending will clearly *lower* the schedule of total spending C + I + G; the rise in taxes on the other hand will reduce the amount of spending that could be devoted by households to consumption and by businessmen to investment So this, too, will contribute to the lowering of the total

FIGURE 13-2

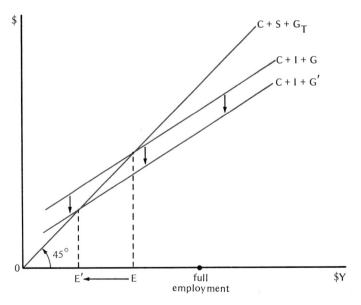

spending schedule C + I + G. The two effects reinforce one another, equilibrium comes at a lower point, and we see that the attempt to balance the budget in a depression, far from helping, has made the depression WORSE, as national income is lowered. The attempts of President Herbert Hoover to ensure that the budget was always balanced from 1930 to 1932, was bad policy which gave an adverse effect; though in fairness it must be said that his successor, Franklin D. Roosevelt, tried to follow the same policy for a long while.

FIGURE 13-3

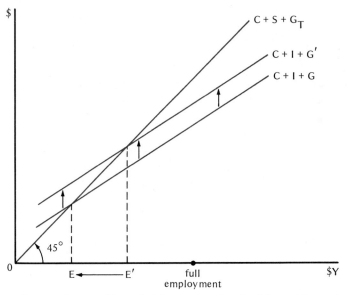

Our understanding of this can be checked by asking what a budget balancing policy will do if the economy begins to enter a period of inflation. As prices and national income rise, an important effect will be that the government's collection of tax revenues will rise in step (Gt up). Another result is that unemployment benefits and agricultural price support payments will decline, meaning government spending (G) is down. If Gt is greater than G, there is a budget surplus. The balancer will therefore want to lower taxes or raise government spending, or both, and Figure 13–3 shows what an abysmal idea that turns out to be. For raising government spending boosts C + I + G directly, while cutting taxes leaves more money available to households who raise their level of consumption, and to businessmen who will be tempted to invest more, and the reinforced result is a new and higher equilibrium giving a higher figure of national income, and thus worsening the inflation.[1]

This does not mean that a balanced budget is NEVER applicable. It might be just the right prescription when the economy is at noninflationary full employment with saving and investment equal. But it is not a cure for depression or inflation, and actually can drive the country deeper into these unhappy areas if employed unwisely.

THE NATIONAL DEBT

At this point we take up a possible deterrent to the use of fiscal policy: the national debt. It should be clear from the case made in the last three chapters that an economic strategy to combat depressions will call for lower taxes or raised government spending or both. This means running a budget deficit, and budget deficits add to the national debt.

You hear a good many arguments on the national debt, and these must be taken up in some detail. For if a debt is quite disadvantageous, then economists will be loathe to use the type of fiscal policy described above to counter depressions.

The position is sometimes taken that the national debt is the same as a private debt—that it is an insupportable burden on the nation's children. If the nation owes over $300 billion dollars, each newborn baby comes into the world owing about $2,000 as his share of the debt. Naturally enough, the cure for all this is not only to keep the debt from rising, but if possible, to reduce it.

The first question to consider is the important one, "Does the cost of government borrowing get passed on to future generations?" It should not take long to show that this is not so in any meaningful sense, and that, in fact, there is no real burden passed on to the nation's children by the national debt. Before you close this book with the shout that ANY debt gets passed on to posterity unless it is paid off, consider the following: public or national debts are different from private and personal debts in at least two areas of vital significance. First of all, governments have the power to tax, and secondly, government bonds, which of course are the national debt, are often much in demand by people who want a safe place to put their money and to earn interest.

So again, to the question, what is the actual burden of the

---

[1]An impact which is amplified by the "multiplier effect" met with earlier.

national debt? We can conceive of a prewar situation where most spending is of the private variety, with some government spending. Should a war come along such as during 1941–45, the government will want to reduce spending in the private sector of the economy and increase it in the public sector, for ships, aircraft, tanks, and so forth. One way this could be accomplished is to raise taxes substantially, thus fighting the war on a pay-as-you-go basis. The difficulty in this is that taxes might have to be raised so high that they dampen the incentive to work. Even red-blooded patriots might not strain that last sinew if they know that most of their earnings will simply be siphoned off by the tax authorities. Thus, taxes are usually raised during hostilities, but not enough to finance the whole war.

Another policy might be for the government to create new money with which to pay its bills (and recall that the sophisticated way to do this is not to print up new paper currency, but to have the Federal Reserve System create demand deposits which can be spent). But this would raise total spending without a corresponding reduction anywhere else, and if the economy started from a position of full employment of men as is expected to be the case in wartime, then this policy would be very inflationary.

A compromise, adopted by the US government as well as most of the other allied and axis nations during World War II, was to sell bonds to citizens. This can be encouraged with "buy War Bonds" propaganda, which is often quite successful. Notice the advantage of this over the two alternatives, taxation and new money. A buyer of bonds has to sacrifice some current consumption to be sure, but he knows that all is not lost to him forever because the bond will earn interest over the years, and eventually in 10 or 20 years' time when it matures, he will be paid the principal in full. Thus incentives are not eroded as they would be by very stiff taxation. On the other hand, when people buy bonds they do, after all, reduce their consumption as noted a moment earlier, and this reduced consumption will tend to offset increased government spending. In Keynesian terms, aggregate demand or total spending will tend to remain unchanged, but the national product can be utilized for military purposes. Then, when the war is over, spending returns to its prewar situation.

All this talk of war is not a flight of fancy, because, as was seen in chapter 12, most of the national debt of the US was incurred to fight World War II. And even in more modern times, the part of the debt not directly attributable to 1941–45 can be largely associated with the Korean and Vietnam conflicts.

Where is the BURDEN of the new national debt? Surely the discussion allows a plain answer. The burden falls in wartime when the debt was accumulated, when people were by choice spending less on themselves and more on government bonds. In a sense, people were buying tanks instead of automobiles, army barracks instead of new houses, flamethrowers instead of electric stoves. It is not only inaccurate, but unfair to the people who sacrifice by buying bonds in wartime, to claim that future generations bear the burden of the national debt. It is borne instead by the people who voluntarily accepted a lower standard of living when the bonds were purchased in the first place.

It is fairly obvious, however, that we have neglected an important consideration. What about the interest payments that must be made yearly on the debt, and which now amount to a full 9% of the government's budget? On the surface this sounds like an enormous burden in its own right, but in fact, the interest on the public debt cannot be considered in the same light as the interest we pay on auto loans or home mortgages. Here is a significant example of how public debt and private debt are not the same thing.

It is true that the government must tax the public to pay interest on the debt once it has been accumulated. That means that in 1970 about $18 billion was extracted from us in taxes to pay this bill. What is often forgotten, however, is that $18 billion is paid right back to us, the American people, because we are the ones who hold the bonds which are the national debt. For the country as a whole, then, there is going to be no net burden of interest payments. Certainly there will be very large sums changing hands in the economy, but only from taxpayer to bondholder with no net loss of output, or purchasing power, or anything else (excluding the much smaller costs of making the transfer).[2] As Abraham Lincoln saw it, as a nation we owe the national debt to ourselves, and it is therefore less worrisome than a very high level of private debt to an individual.

Opponents of a national debt may raise another point: what about the eventual forced repayment of the debt as

---

[2]*Though there may be a redistribution of income, considered subsequently.*

bonds mature over time? Here exactly the same logic is at work as for interest. Certainly we may be taxed to pay off bonds at maturity, but then who gets the payment? The private sector gets taxed; but the private sector *receives the payments in return*. The point was made a few pages earlier that each newborn baby owes about $2000 to the government the moment he enters the world. But is it not just as accurate to say that since the baby belongs to the private sector of the economy, that he is part of the group to which the government OWES $2,000 per person? Hopefully this will clear up some of the confusion that surrounds the whole problem of the national debt.

One point must be added. If by some Herculean feat we should succeed in paying off the whole of the national debt, then what would happen? No bonds where people can sink their savings, no bonds for banks and corporations to buy as an ultra-safe protection for their unused funds, no bonds for the Fed to buy and sell as part of open market operations, the best of the methods to control the nation's money supply. When the US did in fact eliminate its national debt, as in the year 1835 during Jackson's administration, it soon found that wisdom dictated its re-creation. Surely there can be no doubt that the same thing is true of the 1970's.

There are certainly some valid or partially valid objections to a big debt however, which must be kept in mind.

One of the most important objections is that foreigners may hold much of it. This would mean that we are forced to pay *them* the interest and principal on maturity. The net flow of purchasing power beyond the country's borders would then represent a definite sacrifice as people are taxed to pay this interest and principal. Some countries, including Great Britain, have this problem, but fortunately the US does not, as only a very small proportion of our national debt is held by foreigners.

A second objection, valid to some extent, has to do with a possible redistribution of income. If an economy is divided into rich and poor, there might be a suspicion that the rich have purchased the larger amount of bonds. And in addition, if the system of taxation is not based upon ability to pay, that is to say if it is not progressive, then there will be an unfortunate transfer of incomes from poor to rich as taxes are levied to pay the interest on the debt. In the US, due to the loopholes in our tax system, some net redistribution of this type undoubtedly does take place, but not so much as would be the case in a country without the progressive income tax.

The third objection to a high national debt that may be valid to some extent is that the heavy taxation needed to pay the rate of interest will dampen the incentive to work. This is in spite of what we have already said, that this portion of taxes flows back to the economy in any case when the interest on the debt is actually paid. The writer's opinion is that this could possibly be true if taxes were at a very high rate, because of the psychological effect it would bring. But in the US today, we are surely not even close to this position, with only 9¢ out of every tax dollar going to pay interest on the debt. The figure was far higher in the 1940's than it is now.

One last contention remains to be taken up before completing the topic of the national debt. This is that the sheer size of the debt is almost impossible to cope with. As a household or business will eventually go bankrupt if it incurs too many bills, so will the country. This involves a question of fact. Is the debt of the US now larger or smaller in relative terms then it used to be?

Here many readers will probably be surprised, because with the passage of the years the relative size of our debt has been shrinking rather than growing. To prove this, we must first agree that the actual dollar amount of the debt is not a very good measure of our ability to bear it. For example, private debt of $50,000 would be small and give no problems to the Rockefeller family, whereas a debt of only one-tenth that size might bring hardship to a struggling professor of economics.

So it is with countries. A debt is large or small only in relation to the size of the national income; and similarly interest payments on that debt can be called large or small only after considering the size of the national income that can be taxed to pay that interest.

Perhaps some of the most striking statistics on this subject that anyone is likely to encounter can be found in the works of Paul Samuelson, the Nobel Prize winner.[3] Samuelson has constructed a table(reproduced in part here as Table 13–4) showing the national debt in four different years in the first column, the interest on the debt in the second column, and the national income in the third. As we look at the columns, we see that each has grown by very large

---

[3]Paul A. Samuelson, Economics (New York: McGraw-Hill, 8th edition, 1970), p. 344.

TABLE 13–4

	(1) National Debt (billion $)	(2) Interest payments on national debt (billion $)	(3) National Income (billion $)	(4) Size of debt as a percentage of national income	(5) Interest payments on debt as a percentage of national income
Year					
			UNITED STATES		
1868	2.6	0.13	6.8	40%	1.9%
1939	47.6	0.95	72.6	70%	1.3%
1945	278.7	3.66	181.5	150%	2.0%
1970	360	16.5	815	45%	2.0%
			GREAT BRITAIN		
	(1) (billion £)	(2) (billion £)	(3) (billion £)	(4) %	(5) %
1818	0.8	0.031	0.4	210%	7.7%
1923	7.7	0.325	3.95	190%	8.2%
1946	24.0	0.5	8.1	300%	6.2%
1967	32.0	1.2	31.1	100%	3.8%

amounts since 1868; but if we ask ourselves about the percentage importance of the debt in relation to national income between 1868 and 1970, (column four) we discover that, far from presaging some sort of national bankruptcy, the actual size of the debt in 1970 has declined considerably from its 1939 level. It is FAR below the 1945 figure, and is not very far from the 40% of a century ago. Remember also that the period from 1945 to 1970 has been one of great economic growth in this country. In other words, the debt has not caused serious problems to the economy and furthermore it is falling in its proportionate importance.

Now consider column five, which shows interest payments on the debt as a percentage of national income. Here the position is about the same as it was in 1945, and in 1868 as well. There is certainly no tendency here for the relative burden of interest payments to escalate. It is illustrative to note that purely PRIVATE DEBT has increased far, far faster than the national debt in the twenty years after World War II, and is more than two and a half times as big as the latter at about $1.3 trillion in 1970.

The case can go even further than this. Note again that the US national debt is currently 45% of national income, while interest on it is 2% of national income. Then turn to

Samuelson's figures for Great Britain, covering the 150-odd years since 1818. Here we see that British debt has often been two and even three times larger than the national income as compared to our 50% ; while British interest payments have been as high as 8.2% of income compared to our 2%, and even in modern times their figure is about 4%. Someone might be tempted to reply, "But Britain is stagnating, has had to devalue the pound, is economically sick." Perhaps so, but it is impossible to argue that way for the period between 1818 and 1923, when Britain led the world into the Industrial Revolution, when the pound sterling was the standard of excellence among currencies, when Britain in short was *the* major industrial and economic power. These days may be over, but they did after all last for a hundred years. Thus it does not seem plausible to say that the US is overloaded with debt, and the figures shown above make it appear that it could become a great deal larger without becoming unreasonable.

No doubt a national debt would be a terrible problem if the government did not have the power to tax, as was true under the Articles of Confederation in the 1780's. But fortunately we solved that problem in 1789.

Questions

1. Why does a depression or inflation tend automatically to unbalance the budget?
2. What results from an attempt to balance the budget during a depression or inflation?
3. Analyze the arguments against a large and rising national debt. Do some of these arguments have more validity than others?
4. What is the historical evidence concerning whether the US national debt is "too large"?

14.

THE
NEW
ECONOMICS:
A Critical View

The last chapter showed that the problem of the national debt is phantasmagorical, generating fears like "here dwelleth dragons" on the empty spaces of very old maps. Yet there are also difficulties with the Keynesian economics which are far from fully solved. These force us to face some critical problems of economic policy which will remain important issues through the 1970's.

The basic difficulty with the New Economics today is that, although it is capable of coping with all the major problems of economic policy likely to face us, it copes with them at different rates of speed and solves some of these problems before it solves others. And, if pressed far enough to strike at one difficulty, that may mean too much Keynesian medicine for another.

There are four major goals of economic policy, in each of which conflict may appear. First is full employment; second is stability of prices; third is the promotion of long-term economic growth for the economy, and fourth is the avoidance of balance of payments problems in the international sphere.[1]

---

[1]One of these goals, full employment, has even been spelled out by congress in the Employment Act of 1946.

In the course of the book, employment and prices have been considered at some length; while growth and the balance of payments have so far received little attention. In what follows the unfortunate fact will become apparent that the prescriptions of the New Economics tend sometimes to come into conflict in all these areas.

FULL EMPLOYMENT

Take employment first. Our schedules of total spending have often pictured full employment as a point along the horizontal axis of our diagrams. There is a difficulty with a simple picture like this, however. At any period of time there will be two types of unemployment that cannot be immediately eliminated by raising total spending (or aggregate demand) in the economy, thus giving enough production so that everyone can have a job. The first type is the so-called "frictional" unemployment, which means that at any time some people will be changing jobs or just entering the job market, and temporarily these people will have to be listed as out of work.

Secondly there is "structural" unemployment, which means that some workers without skills or education will not be unemployed because there are no jobs to be had, but instead because these jobs require a certain minimum of skill. So the fact must be faced that there will always be some unemployment, both frictional and structural, which will not be wholly eliminated by the Keynesian policy of raising aggregate demand. It is thought that perhaps 3 to 4% of the labor force is in this situation in the US.[2] On the other hand, all unemployment above this level ought to be nicely handled by the New Economics, while for frictional or structural unemployment, government programs such as retraining, travel and housing allowances, and so forth, can greatly lessen the unpleasantness of unemployment. Great Britain, West Germany, and France all have good records on this score, but Sweden leads the western world in coping with frictional and structural unemployment, as will be explored in chapter 15.

---

[2] In recent years, 4% has become the more accepted figure. Secretary of the Treasury Connally at a news conference in July, 1971 argued vehemently that even 4% is too low a figure for frictional and structural unemployment.

PRICE STABILITY

But there is the other big problem of price stability, and here is the first conflict. Up to now we have been operating under a simple assumption. If during depression when unemployment is present, national income begins to grow, then prices remain stable until full employment is reached, and then *at* full employment any further increase in income will be inflationary, with rising prices. In fact, however, experience shows that this assumption is not quite correct. As national income begins to rise at the end of a period of deflation, and as the economy nears full employment, almost always prices are expected to rise BEFORE full employment is achieved. One reason this might happen is that shortages or bottlenecks may develop in some industries and markets before others. Say the copper industry gets overstrained before full employment is reached everywhere; or the market for trained engineers gets very tight. Both bottlenecks could well cause prices to start rising before the entire economy comes to a position of full employment.

Right there is the conflict. Really full employment can be achieved only at the price of a certain degree of inflation. In terms of American experience, it appears that economic policy if managed correctly can effectively prevent *serious* depressions and inflations. When smaller doses of the two ills are present, however, the problem is more intractable. To repeat, modern experience shows that it is not possible, using standard fiscal and monetary policy, to completely eliminate unemployment without starting a rise in prices.[3]

There have been many suggestions both here and abroad as to how to solve this difficulty, (one was the Nixon package of August, 1971) and these are also considered in chapter 15.

---

[3]*This is often called the problem of the "trade-off" between unemployment and inflation. Recent investigations in papers published by the prestigious Brookings Institution suggest that to cool off inflation to an annual level of 3% would require that we put up with a high 5.2% rate of unemployment. Many economists feel that, with growing requirements for education and skills, with more teen-agers and women in the labor force, etc., the trade-off situation is worse than it was in the mid-1950's. For that earlier date, it is suggested that a 3% rate of inflation could have been achieved with only 4% unemployment.*

LONG-TERM ECONOMIC GROWTH

The third item in our list of objectives, long-term economic growth, may also involve a conflict. To promote growth, we would undoubtedly want to encourage *investment* above all, as that will give us the bigger stock of capital which will help to increase future production. Investment can be supported directly by tax credits such as President Kennedy's 1962 measures,[4] or indirectly by keeping aggregate demand close to full employment to ensure the profitability of businessmen's investment projects, and keeping interest rates low. Some people think that a little inflation is even better for growth, but that position is far from completely convincing. Even so, something of a conflict between growth and price stability will have to be considered, because promoting growth via a high level of aggregate demand may tend to be inflationary, and this would be fueled by low interest rates.

Fortunately, growth can also be promoted in other ways. Better training and education, better management techniques, encouragement of new and more productive methods of doing things, all help the process, and it does not appear that these *will* conflict seriously with an economy's other aims.

BALANCE OF PAYMENTS

The last of the goals a modern economy seeks, is a trouble-free balance of payments in international trade. The balance of payments is merely a way of describing the fact that a country must sell abroad as much as it buys, or it must find someone to extend it credit. Think of all the ways a nation can acquire money from abroad. It can export goods, it can perform services such as providing shipping or insurance, or housing and feeding foreign tourists, its citizens can receive pensions from foreign governments or companies, or it can persuade foreigners to invest their funds in American business; either directly by starting up or expanding foreign-owned business, or by purchasing American stocks and bonds. Finally, foreigners may put their money in banks, in New York or elsewhere, because they think dollars are more secure than French francs and whatnot, or that their money will earn higher rates of interest in American banks, etc.

---

4 *And a similar plan, not yet adopted, which was attracting wide criticism in 1971.*

Then take the mirror image of this. Think of all the ways *foreigners* can acquire American dollars. When Americans import foreign goods, or use foreign shipping or airlines or insurance, when we travel abroad, when our government gives foreign aid or pays pensions, when our citizens send gifts back to the old country, or when Americans invest abroad by buying stocks or bonds, or set up their own businesses, or send dollars to Switzerland where they are exchanged for Swiss francs and kept on deposit because it is thought that the dollar is unsafe, or that interest rates are higher abroad.

If these two do not balance out; that is, if we spend more abroad than foreigners spend here or vice-versa, then the balance of payments is not in equilibrium. If we spend more abroad than foreigners spend here in the course of a year, we will end up on balance owing foreigners money. This is called a balance of payments deficit, and the US was headed for its worst deficit in history during 1971—a prime catalyst for the August emergency measures and the December devaluation. If we spend less abroad than foreigners spend here, then we end up being owed money and that is termed a balance of payments surplus. West Germany and Japan are the countries which have had the largest surpluses in recent years.

If a country has a surplus, there is no immediate cause for it to worry even though its trading partners will automatically have to be running a deficit. But the country in deficit will have to pay its bills in some way. The most familiar means of settling international accounts is by transfers of gold. If the US ends up owing money to France, one way the debt can be settled is by shipping part of the American gold stock to Paris.[5] However, anyone could understand that *this* method of settling a debt is going to be a temporary one, strictly limited by the amount of gold a country has stockpiled. We should be well aware of this, seeing that the American gold stock has been approximately cut in half in recent years.[6]

The other way out is by obtaining credit from foreign countries. Over the past eight to ten years, a wide network of

---

[5] *Or, as is more commonly done, transferring the ownership title on gold kept in the United States from the U.S. to France.*

[6] *It was worth over $20 billion in the late 1950's, only $10.5 billion now. The US did not any longer pay with gold, except to a very minor degree, even before the August 1971 reforms.*

official and semi-official credit has developed; currency "swaps" as they are called between governments, loans from the International Monetary Fund, and so on. Here, too, it should be fairly obvious that nations will not extend credit forever. As a temporary measure, yes, but the time will have to come when a nation must pay its bills or the credit will stop. So given a balance of payments deficit, when the US is buying and investing more abroad than foreigners are spending or investing here, it is plain that handling this via outflows of gold *or* via credit are going to be essentially short-term.

So, what can be done to get the balance of payments back into balance during a time of deficit? Perhaps the crudest and easiest to understand of the methods is to slap tariffs (which are simply taxes) on imported goods. Perhaps quotas, too, can be used. Quotas are a device to set a maximum level on imports. Combined with controls on investment, on travel abroad, and others, our foreign spending can be strictly limited, thus bringing the balance of payments back to equilibrium. Unfortunately, however, tariffs and all the rest are not a very happy alternative. They tend to provoke retaliatory action from trading partners. If the US puts a tariff on French wines, then France puts a tariff on goods IT imports from this country, and no one is any better off—least of all the con- sumers in France and America who end up paying higher prices because of the tariffs. No, this simply will not do, because if used to any degree, as in the 1930's, it will set off a war of tariff and counter-tariff that leaves trade in a shambles and is of no benefit to anyone.[7]

Another step might be the familiar one of devaluing the currency. If it is announced that instead of exchanging US dollars for French francs at 1 dollar = 5 francs, in the future the US will exchange at 1 dollar = 3 francs, this makes the dollar less valuable in relation to the franc. The same decision is

---

[7]*Tariffs and quotas have another grave disadvantage. They are legislated by Congress on specifically named goods. Thus, industries with strong political leverage tend to build themselves strong protective barriers (such as oil and steel), while industries with less influence go without tariffs and quotas. This is a haphazard state of affairs, often highly discriminatory and in the author's opinion usually indefensible. The 10% "border tax" of August 1971 is really a comprehensive tariff on all imports, and although it is subject to the disadvantages of foreign retaliation, it does at least avoid the problem on inter-industry discrimination mentioned in this footnote.*

made for the exchange rate between the dollar and all other currencies. Thus we have devalued.[8]

What does this mean for trade? First, Americans find it more expensive to buy French goods, travel there, invest there, and so forth. Where each dollar used to get us five francs worth of French goods, we get only three francs worth now. So we cut down our purchases abroad. On the other hand, foreigners discover that the dollar is cheaper for them. A Frenchman, for example, can buy a dollar's worth of American goods for only 3 francs, instead of 5, so foreigners *increase* their purchases in this country. Thus devaluation appears to be a sound solution; but devaluation is politically bad for a government because it is often regarded as the sign of a weak economy, and particularly in the case of the US, many foreign countries have large holdings of dollars which they use along with gold to pay off their international obligations. If we devalued the dollar, these foreign governments would find the value of the dollars they hold has been cut. For years the US therefore insisted that it would stay clear of devaluation. Lastly, there is the ever-present danger that one devaluation could start a round of competitive devaluations on the part of other countries as well. Any time a major country devalues, some, perhaps dozens, of other countries may be tempted to devalue as well, so as not to lose their competitive advantage. For these reasons, the US avoided devaluation as a means to balance of payments equilibrium for so long, only to be pushed into it in December, 1971.

---

[8]*The effect of a devaluation (or its reverse, an upward revaluation) can be obtained through a device known as a "floating" exchange rate. In the example above, it was an explicit government decision to devalue which resulted in changing the dollar-franc rate from 1 to 5 to 1 to 3. "Floating" a currency is different; it means allowing market forces to determine its price, just as, for example, market forces determine the price of wheat. When wheat is in great supply and not in much demand, its price will be low, and high when the situation is reversed. Correspondingly, when the dollar is "floating" a glut of dollars and little demand for them among foreigners will cause the price of dollars (expressed in francs or other foreign currencies) to fall. A floating rate can thus give the same effect as a devaluation if a currency is too weak. Floating rates have not been much used in modern times among major nations. The Canadian dollar floated during the 1950's while the German mark and Netherlands guilder have been floated for short periods in recent years. International bankers, merchants, and many government officials tend in particular to dislike floating rates because (like wheat prices) they might change from day-to-day and thus complicate the task of foreign trade. It was therefore a major shock, to foreigners especially, when President Nixon announced a floating US dollar in August 1971.*

The last way by which the balance of payments may be adjusted ought to have a familiar ring. That is by altering total spending and consequently national income in a country. It ought to be fairly easy to show that raising or lowering the level of national income will have an impact on foreign trade. For example, imports are for the most part simply consumption goods produced abroad; and like domestic consumption, imports will vary greatly according to whether income and spending are high or low in an economy. Take a rising level of national income. This is almost certain to bring a rising amount of imports, as people have more money to spend and choose to spend part of it on foreign goods. The opposite is true also: a falling national income ought to mean, and experience shows that it does mean, a reduction in a country's imports.

Therefore, the tools of the New Economics are available to adjust the balance of payments. Fiscal policy and monetary policy can both be employed to raise or lower the national income, and hence to raise or lower the level of imports in an attempt to bring the balance of payments back into equilibrium.

Fine, then—even if we do not want to use tariffs, and are against devaluation, we still have an easy way to solve our international problems. Deficits, the loss of gold, scrounging around to find governments or international agencies which will extend us credit, can all be dispensed with if Keynesian policy is used to control the level of national income so that the balance of payments is in equilibrium.

But one crucial point has been neglected. If the national income is cut to reduce imports, or if it is raised to encourage imports, this might just possibly run afoul of our other three goals, full employment, price stability, and growth. A little thought will lead to the conclusion that such a policy might not be compatible with full employment. Take an exchange rate such as Great Britain's until 1967. One British Pound Sterling was worth two dollars and eighty cents in American currency. At that rate, it might have been true that a national income high enough to give full employment, would also be so high as to promote an excess of imports over and above Britain's exports; that is, a balance of payments deficit. There are three solutions, as we discussed earlier. The government might slap on tariffs, quotas, or other controls, but Britain did not want to do that, because of international obligations and because she feared foreign retaliation. Then she might devalue her currency, down to something like one pound equalling two dollars and forty cents—as eventually happened. But *this* she wanted to fight to the last ditch, particularly since many foreign governments held pounds, with dollars and gold, as part of their country's reserves, and secondly because, from a political point of view, it was thought by many that Britain's prestige would fall if she were to devalue.

So that left the New Economics. A nation can cut down the level of imports, as already noted, by deflating the economy so that there is less income with which to purchase imports. That is exactly what Britain did, time after time in the ten years before 1967. She would tighten the screws of monetary and fiscal policy in order to deflate the economy, lower the level of imports, and bring the balance of payments into equilibrium. It is not difficult to see what happened when this policy was tried. At every turn of the deflationary screw, with national income being restrained, a tendency was revealed for some extra unemployment to develop. Whether the party in power was the Conservative or the Labor Party, political brows were marked with political furrows, and the deflationary restraint was ended to boost employment figures again. Then, of course, this in turn would lead right back to the starting point; a nice low level of unemployment, but the balance of payments back in the red.

In an automotive sense, there was a continuous process of putting on the gas only to shift right over to the brake, and the British coined a phrase to describe the muddle: the STOP-GO it was called. The British finally did devalue their currency as we know, and they hope that the bad old days of stop-go are over. Perhaps that will turn out to be correct, though their rapid rate of inflation in 1970–1971 does not bode well.

The reason for bringing this up is not simply to illustrate the problems of a foreign country, however interesting that may be, but rather because the US was in that position in 1971 . A decade ago we had few problems of this sort. But, in recent years, we have made the discovery that at or near full employment in this country, our balance of payments is very likely to be in deficit at the rates of exchange in existence up to August, 1971.[9]

---

[9]*Although only the preliminary figures for 1971 are available, at the moment of writing it looks as if the US balance of payments deficit for that year will be the largest ever recorded.*

The US government insisted for years, as this dilemma grew, that it would not devalue the dollar. As a result, very strong protectionist noises emanated from congress in 1970–71. Most informed people, however, were too sensible to want to cure the problem with tariffs and quotas. Recall that foreigners would be expected to retaliate, leaving us no better off than we were. In any case, tariffs are just a sales tax, and a very haphazard one at that, on the goods that the consumer buys.

So that leaves the New Economics again, with the US by 1971 in much the same dilemma that Great Britain was in. We could cure the balance of payments problem by deflating, but if we started at noninflationary full-employment, then we would end up with some extra unemployment, with all the difficulties that entails.

As events showed in August and December, 1971, we did not choose the route of deflation. But floating currencies and the eventual dollar devaluation pose problems of their own for economists and economically literate citizens.

SUMMARY

Whether the New Economics can eventually cope with the difficult questions of conflict posed in this chapter is a point of continuing debate. Another quarter century will see many experiments and presumably some successes. New thinking and experimentation is already under way as seen in the August, 1971, measures, and in a number of foreign countries, and this is taken up in the concluding chapter, which follows.

Questions

1. What are the major conflicts which arise in modern economic policy-making?
2. Would we ever expect a zero rate of unemployment?
3. What is the STOP-GO?
4. What ways can you suggest to eliminate a balance of payments deficit?

15.

THE
NEW
ECONOMICS:
Experiments

This chapter consists of a look at the major experiments being conducted here and abroad to solve the economic problems presented in the last chapter, and emphasizes the remarkable changes in economic policy implemented in this country in August, 1971.

EXPERIMENTS

No puzzle of economic management has been more perplexing nor generated more political ill-will, than the occurrence simultaneously of unemployment and inflationary price-rises. As of early 1971, unemployment was about 6%—the highest since the early 1960's.[1] Meanwhile inflation through the twelve months of 1970 was percolating along at about 5%.

The Nixon administration pushed diligently since 1969 to remedy this, but success was elusive. Even Mr. Nixon's steady conversion to Keynesian economics did not solve the dilemma. As late as his message accompanying the fiscal 1971 budget, he

---

[1]Capacity utilization in manufacturing was 73% in early 1971, lower even than during the recession of 1958.

spoke of the desirability of a balanced budget. However, by January, 1971, Mr. Nixon had announced his adherence to the doctrines of Keynesian economics, and his fiscal 1972 budget certainly sounded like the New Economics. He insisted on the "determination of the federal government to take an activist role,"[2] and spoke of full-employment budgeting.[3]

In spite of this conversion to Keynes, the combination of unemployment-cum-inflation proved very stubborn.[4] The Nixon administration's "Game Plan" called for tight monetary and fiscal policy to fight the inflation (a traditional Keynesian approach). By 1971, with another presidential election in the distance and inflation continuing to act up, it was clear that the high level of unemployment still afflicting the economy was politically unacceptable. Thus during 1971, the authorities permitted rapid monetary growth and an expansionary fiscal deficit was allowed to develop. (The administration had originally planned a $1.3 billion surplus for the fiscal year 1971,[5] a long step from the deficit of over $20 billion that appears likely to be recorded after all the figures are in. Thus it is hardly surprising that attention has focused on experiments by which new methods of controlling this situation can be developed. Below, the economics of these methods are examined, and followed by an analysis of the surprising measures adopted in August, 1971.

PRICES AND INCOMES POLICIES

No experiment in modern economic management has

2Newsweek, Feb. 8, 1971, p. 68.
3A concept in which deficit spending is planned for whenever unemployment exceeds some minimal level. The Nixon administration's minimal level has been about 4%. (Recall Secretary Connally's objection to this figure, mentioned in chapter 13).
4Experience during other inflations has shown that when using monetary and fiscal policies as measures of control, the inflation tends to persist even after the economy has cooled off and unemployment has started to mount. The decline in business activity as tight government policies take hold may cause businessmen's costs to rise (e.g., higher taxes, higher interest rates), while wages continue up because of union contracts negotiated earlier in the inflation. This situation is only temporary, but it is discouraging while it lasts. A case in point is the 1957–1958 recession in the US.
5July 1, 1970 to June 30, 1971.

attracted more comment than so-called "prices and incomes policies." In the 1960's, with several countries suffering from too much inflation *and* at the same time too much unemployment, the idea gained currency that the introduction of controls, perhaps even a "freeze," on the prices of goods and services and the factors of production, might keep them from rising before full employment is reached.

In this country, an early and fairly feeble attempt, now defunct, was made by President Johnson who suggested norms for price increases, called guidelines. In Great Britain and elsewhere in western Europe, on the other hand, these policies have been tried at some length and provide interesting evidence of this alternative way to obtain full employment without setting off a price rise.[6] Yet it cannot really be said that the experience of prices and incomes policies in Europe has been very good. They have had some success in the Netherlands and Sweden, have had their problems in France, and have failed utterly in Britain. Perhaps the concern most often voiced is if prices and incomes are controlled for very long, how then will the prices of goods or the wages of labor continue to reflect actual scarcity in the economy? Rising prices or wages do, after all, play the important role in a market system of signalling where scarcity is appearing, and attracting new resources into the area. Take beef prices among a myriad of possible examples. Higher prices here, instead

---

[6]*There were straws in the wind for many months before the US adopted its own such policy in August, 1971. In June, 1970, the President initiated a new system of "Inflation Alerts," whereby attention could be called to inflationary price or wage increases. As these alerts came only after the event they described, they were far different from the prices and incomes policies in use abroad. Arthur Burns, Chairman of the Fed's Board of Governors, was one of the most prominent Americans arguing for a strong incomes policy here. This even caused something of a rift between Burns and President Nixon because of the latter's uncompromising rejection of wage–price controls in his public utterances through July of 1971. In that month, political commentators and economists generally seemed to think that the most radical policy likely to be adopted would be something similar to a plan suggested by Gardner Ackley, who was chairman of President Johnson's Council of Economic Advisors. He advocated the establishment of a new high-level wage and price review board, independent of the President. Ackley suggested that the board would receive prior notice of wage and price increases and have the power to halt these for a limited period. This proposal (which went beyond Arthur Burns' arguments), has some similarity to the "Prices and Incomes Board" which ruled on British price and wage increases during the late 1960's.*

of being part of a general inflation, may be the warning that beef production is dropping, or that consumers are shifting away from other meats and towards steak. Thus the rising beef price may lead ranchers to raise more steers, tending to alleviate the shortage. This mechanism becomes less effective the more controls are placed on prices. (The same argument applies to wages as a measure of the scarcity of labor of a particular type.)[7]

In Great Britain, prices and incomes policy collapsed in 1969, and the major reason for the collapse seems clear. The policy must have wide national support, or the party in office will not have the fortitude to withstand the strikes of labor unions or the sniping of business associations opposed to the scheme.

The British government was faced with strikes for higher wages by unions which could have caused a breakdown in public services. The industries affected included the railways, hospital workers, teachers, garbage collectors, and others. Rather than face strikes in these areas, the government gave in, permitting large wage increases. All proponents of a prices and incomes policy must consider the British failure, for in the US too, governments (federal, state and local) have often struggled to avoid strikes in public service industries. Some further comments on prices and incomes policies are included in the last section of this chapter, which discusses the "New Nixon Game Plan."

FEDERAL EMPLOYMENT

Another possible way out of the inflation-unemployment dilemma is federal employment: one such plan was suggested recently by Professor Mel Ulmer of the University of Maryland.[8] Ulmer believes that a new national agency, taking over present programs for welfare and unemployment benefits, should also institute wide-ranging programs for retraining. Unemployed

---

[7]Though, as Professor P.M. Hohenberg of Cornell University pointed out in The New York Times during August 1971, it is too often true that even without government price regulations, prices may be tacitly controlled by monopolistic elements in the corporate structure (steel, oil, automobiles, cigarettes, etc.). Thus the choice is not necessarily between controls and no controls.
[8]Melville J. Ulmer, The Welfare State (Boston: Houghton Mifflin Co., 1969).

workers could benefit from this retraining, intended to be on a broader scale than that involved in present programs. The new agency would include a computerized job matching center, which on a national basis, would match unemployed workers with vacancies. For those unemployed workers who do not successfully complete the retraining program, the agency will have one final responsibility. It will act as an "employer of last resort," with the task of providing useful employment in such possible areas as highway beautification, ghetto rehabilitation, national park improvement, and other socially neglected areas.

Ulmer's plan would have the advantage, when compared to both the present situation and to a proposed prices and incomes policy, of allowing monetary and fiscal policy to be pressed hard against inflation, but with the resulting unemployment sopped up by the new government agency.[9]

Some foreign experience in this area is noteworthy. For example, the Swedish government runs 24 regional and 600 local employment offices which provide job information, including a 60-page weekly gazette of work openings. Retraining courses which provide needed skills last from 12 weeks to two years, with the trainee's expenses paid for by the government. Generous allowances for travel to and settling in new areas are available, and the Swedish authorities will even purchase the worker's former house if no other buyer can be found, to ensure that no unemployed person is trapped in an area with few job opportunities. Many of these ideas are being heard in the US Congress nowadays, and some are likely to be adopted here.

TAX PENALTIES

A final alternate possibility in the control of inflation and unemployment was suggested in the fall of 1970 by Professors Henry Wallich of Yale University and Sidney Weintraub of the University of Pennsylvania, and was a variant type of

---

[9] *A bill incorporating some of these points was passed by Congress but vetoed by President Nixon near year's end, 1970. In the summer of 1971, a substitute $2 billion bill was again passaged by Congress, and this time was not vetoed. However, the bill is much less comprehensive then Ulmer's proposal.*

prices and incomes policy. Wallich and Weintraub feel that a special tax could be levied on businesses which raise prices after granting especially inflationary wage increases because of strong union demands. This would have the effect of generating business resistance to wage increases, not now present where price hikes are easy.

President Nixon's administration had little enthusiasm for any of these experiments, but with the situation showing no improvement in the summer of 1971 and with the 1972 election approaching, the administration was under heavy pressure to adopt a new stance toward these proposals.

MONETARY EXPERIMENTS

Another area of experimentation has been monetary policy.[10] Here, some foreign central banks have been very active in trying to promote economic growth while at the same time restraining the possible inflationary impact of that growth, via channeling funds into priority uses. Special lower discount rates or partial exemption from reserve requirements on loans are granted to sectors such as housing, agriculture, growth industries, exports, and state and local government. At least two of these priority sectors receive special benefits from the Banque de France, the Reserve Bank of India, the Banca d'Italia, the Nihon Ginko (which is the central bank of Japan), the Banco de Mexico, the Sveriges Riksbank in Sweden, and the Deutsche Bundesbank in Germany. All five of the priority sectors are aided in France, Japan, and Mexico. This is to be contrasted with the Federal Reserve System in the US, where the Fed does not provide special support in these areas.

Some central banks have developed "moral suasion" much more than has the Fed in this country. It appears to have far greater impact in Great Britain, Italy, and Sweden, in the latter of which there is an "annual credit agreement" between the central bank and the commercial banks as to the type of loans that should be made (and avoided) during the coming year.

The most active use of monetary policy, far exceeding the

---

[10]See "Commentary on Central Bank Activities," Business Conditions (Federal Reserve Bank of Chicago, April, 1971).

employment of fiscal policy, has been in Japan. Here, Nihon Ginko has built the discount rate into a very important weapon of control, and uses it almost ruthlessly to control inflations and recessions.

Innovations in the area of standard fiscal policy have already been covered in some detail in chapters 11 and 12 where the possibilities of a shelf of public works projects and more rapid changes in tax rates were emphasized. This discussion need not be repeated here.

"PEACE AND PROSPERITY" THE NEW NIXON GAME PLAN

On Sunday evening, August 14, 1971, President Nixon announced a new economic game plan which he said was designed to achieve prosperity in a peace-time economy and which has been rightly called the most surprising turnabout in US economic management in forty years. The shock of the emergency measures was all the more intense because the administration spokesmen had been reiterating their determination to hold to the old game plan of standard monetary and fiscal policy, *sans* controls, devaluation, or any of the other experiments discussed in this chapter.

The measures are wide-ranging, in fact, more comprehensive than those being suggested just before their imposition, by the vast majority of economists and politicians. Below, each new policy is described, linked to the area in this chapter where such reforms were discussed in general, and then analyzed critically.

1. *The wage-price freeze.* Controls on wages and prices are not new. Both were established at fixed levels in the ancient Babylonian Empire by the Code of Hammurabi about 2100 BC. In the Roman Empire, the edict of 301 A.D. under Diocletian was even more comprehensive. In the US the two most recent freezes were during World War II and the Korean war. Rapid inflation (running over 12% per year) following the Pearl Harbor attack led to controls in April 1942, lasting until November, 1946. Equally high inflation at the end of 1950, due to the Korean war, caused controls to be adopted in

January, 1951. They were removed by President Eisenhower in 1953.

The August 1971 wage-price freeze was different in some respects. For one thing, it was a short-term freeze (90 days). It was also not backed by a huge bureaucracy, such as the Office of Price Administration (OPA) of 1942–46 or the Office of Price Stabilization (OPS) of the early 1950's. Still, it was hardly "voluntary" as administration spokesmen have claimed, as the freeze was backed by the power to fine for non-compliance. Interestingly, the legislation empowering the President to declare a freeze was passed by a Democratic Congress in 1970 over the administration's protests that such legislation was unnecessary. A new body, the Cost of Living Council, with Treasury Secretary Connally as its chairman, administered the program.

Another difference is that the freeze was not being imposed to stop a sudden spurt of war-induced inflation. It was intended instead to halt a slower degree of inflation without causing the trade-off rise in unemployment that we have come to expect from the more conventional anti-inflationary weapons.

Specific criticism of the August 1971 freeze has focused on the problem of equity, because not all forms of income were included. For example, neither interest nor dividends and other profits were controlled. The administration countered that present legislation did not allow the freeze to be extended to these areas, but eventually the President requested Congress to pass some such enabling legislation. Several economists have recommended an excess-profits tax to rectify this situation.

One thing should be made quite clear. A freeze does not eliminate the causes of an inflation. It simply hides them, pushing them under the rug, so to speak. When a freeze ends inflation will simply perk along again unless in the meantime new reforms are made. That is why "Phase Two" of the new game plan contains other controls on wages and prices— not a freeze this time, but something like the old guidelines for increases.

The final powers of the bodies which administer the "unfrozen" Phase Two of the new economic game plan were still not entirely clear as this book went to press.

However, by December 1971, several details were in place.

A "Pay Board" with tripartite labor, management, and public representatives sitting on it was in charge of administering wage increases, while price increases were to be overseen by a "Price Commission" whose members all were from the general public.

Meanwhile, Secretary Connally's Cost of Living Council was still in existence, and debate centered on whether it would have a veto power on the decisions of the Price Commission and, more particularly, the Pay Board. These latter two were to have authority to establish guidelines for permissible, and presumably noninflationary, wage and price increases.

2. *The floating dollar, the 10% border tax, and the devaluation.* To counter the fast deteriorating US balance of payments position, the President floated the dollar and imposed an immediate 10% border tax on most imports. Both of these devices for economic management have already been examined. (See Chapter 13.) Both were in essence ways of devaluing the dollar without explicitly calling it a devaluation. It was fully anticipated that the 10% import surcharge would eventually be removed in the bargaining with other nations for a return to fixed exchange rates, and this in fact took place in December, 1971. Following a series of conferences, the dollar was devalued about 8% vis à vis many currencies, the impact of which was even greater in the cases of the Japanese yen and the German mark, which were revalued upward at the same time.

3. *The new fiscal measures.* The changes announced by President Nixon in the area of fiscal policy are for this author perhaps the least convincing. Heading the list is a so-called "job development tax credit" of 10%. Behind this sonorous phrase is nothing more than the old investment tax credit, originally instituted by President Kennedy, which has been criticized for its generosity to business. The accompanying proposal to increase income tax exemptions by $50.00 in 1972 instead of in 1973 as originally planned is by no means as generous for the consuming public. Meanwhile, the President announced two other fiscal moves: a 10% reduction in foreign aid and a 5% reduction in federal employment. The careful reader of this book should note immediately the inconsistency here. On the tax side, the new fiscal measures are expansionary;

on the spending side they will engineer a contraction. Once again we see the old shibboleth of the balanced budget, which, as pointed out in chapters 12 and 13 still has great political impact.

The reader should understand that the actual structure of all these new measures is of less importance than the long-awaited firm decision of government to institute a program of peace-time controls. In the months and years to come, the framework described above will undoubtedly be altered to take account of the lessons of experience. And Congress or the Courts may change the final appearance of Phase Two.

The critical question, however, is whether the US experiments in the area of controls will fare better than they have abroad. Economic history warns us to be pessimistic; the life of such programs has often been all too short because public confidence in them ebbs, and the will to enforce them against strong labor unions and united management ebbs likewise. Only time, the great teacher, will tell.

SUMMARY

Amid this welter of experimentation, one statement can be made which will stand as a final summary for the book. Though many problems of economic management remain unsolved the principles of the Keynesian economics do give western market economics the needed weapons to do battle with really serious inflations and depressions. Correct use of monetary and fiscal policy should ensure that virulent cases of these diseases will not recur in well-managed economies. True, we struggle along with some inflation, unemployment, perhaps even slow growth and balance of payments difficulties. Experimentation to eliminate these annoying problems has proceeded rapidly. Each of the new plans has its adherents, but none appears to be a panacea. It is obvious that the meshing of full employment, price stability, growth, and a satisfactory balance of payments is at once more complex and more difficult than was thought to be the case a few years ago. But fortunately this situation is an immense improvement over the great "booms and busts" of capitalism in its classical era—the control of which is our legacy from John Maynard Keynes.

Questions

1. What is a "prices and incomes policy"?
2. What are its advantages and disadvantages?
3. What other experiments have been suggested in economic management?
4. What is your opinion of the August 1971 measures?

16.

RESUME

There is no doubt that the "classic" economics failed to cope with a grave historical deficiency in economic management. Throughout its history, capitalism as an economic system has been beset by a serious continuing cycle of booms and slumps, the one following the other, sometimes prolonged, sometimes not so bad, but almost as regular as death and taxes.

We saw that this statement does not convey the human cost involved, because a slump (the worst offender) brings with it the scourge of unemployment, mortgages foreclosed, accumulated savings destroyed, business failures, and the growth of the economy halted. A boom may not be much better. For booms may bring with them inflation, and if the inflation is serious then people on fixed incomes—the elderly, for example —find themselves ever worse off as prices rise; the value of savings is eroded. The whole psychology of a nation may turn away from real economic growth and focus itself on speculation to keep up with rising prices.

John Maynard Keynes, later Lord Keynes, of Cambridge University in England, was the man whose book of 1936, *The General Theory*, plus uncounted subsequent investigations by Keynes and his followers, gave us the New Economics. This, in turn, provides methods of coping with the age-old problems of inflation and depression.

Any theory which describes the behavior of an economy must involve at the same time an adequate system of measurement so that the investigator can tell what is happening *to* that economy. A brainchild of Keynesianism was the development of several ways to measure total output and income during a given year. The most familiar of these is the Gross National Product, which represents during one year the nation's production of goods and services. Some of these goods and services are for consumption, some add to the nation's stock of man-made capital and receive the label investment, and some are goods and services acquired by the government.

In calculating national product, care must be taken never to count items more than once. It is not permissible to include the value of all bread produced, all flour produced, and all wheat produced, because a good deal of the flour and wheat in value terms, are already included with the bread. In other words, avoid double counting.

Other transactions are merely transfers, such as gifts, sale of stocks and bonds, sale of second-hand goods, etc., which do not represent the production of new goods or services. These, too, must be excluded.

There is another way to look at the national product, and in concept the money amount will be identical, barring a minor exception or two. In producing any item, factors of production must be hired: these are land (including natural resources), labor, capital, and entrepreneurial ability (the entrepreneur, recall, is the man who does the initiating, organizing, and risk-taking). Incomes are earned by these factors; rent for land, wages and salaries for labor, interest on capital, and profit as the return to the entrepreneur. It was shown that if a product which sells for $100 is produced, then the factors of production will have earned $100 as their return—some for the land, labor, and capital, and whatever is left over as profit for the entrepreneur. Thus income earned from the sale of an item is identical to the market price at which the item is sold. Therefore, the national income of a country is the same conceptually as the national product.

There are other measures of income and product in common use in the US, including net national product, personal income, and disposable personal income. Yet even this proliferation does not protect us completely against unthinking use of product and income statistics. They are a far from perfect measure of well-being, and are subject to error in making comparisons either over time or between countries. Some of the major problems are size of the population, changes in the price level, and the distribution of income.

The basis of the Keynesian New Economics is the equilibrium level of national income. In any market economy there are forces at work which will determine the level of national income and determine whether it rises or falls.

In the absence of government (not far wrong, economically speaking, for the period before the 1930's) the crucial relationship is between total spending in the economy and total output, or to put it another way, "Will there be enough spending in an economy to buy up all the output produced in a given year?"

Keynes concentrated on the way in which spending and output can be divided. Take spending first. With government and foreign trade omitted, the two possibilities open are to spend on consumption (C) or to spend on investment goods (I). Total spending is thus $C + I$.

What about the nation's output, which, as noted a few paragraphs above, is equivalent to the incomes earned in the production of that output? This can be conveniently divided into the two ways in which income can be used, government and foreign trade still omitted. Households can use their income for consumption (C) or can save it (S). Thus, total output and hence income, equals $C + S$.

If we want total spending to be just high enough to buy up the nation's output, then $C + I$ will have to equal $C + S$. For an economy to be in equilibrium, therefore, with no pressure for change in income and output being generated, then total spending or aggregate demand, $C + I$ must be exactly equal to total output and income, sometimes called aggregate supply, $C + S$.

We discussed what it is that determines each of these important variables of the New Economics. Consumption and saving are linked closely to the level of income—the higher the income, the more C and S. Thus the opinion of the classical economists—that saving is closely connected to the rate of interest—was not correct.

What determines investment? Businessmen invest in order to obtain profit, which in turn, depends on their expectation of business conditions in the economy, and more debatably the rate of interest they will have to pay on the money they borrow to finance the investment project.

What would happen if for some reason, starting with total spending C + I equal to total output and income C + S, national product rises but businessmen want to invest what they had been investing before? If this is true, then spending C + I MUST be less than output C + S.

This will, in turn, be noticed by businessmen. For of necessity it means that there is not enough spending to buy up all the output produced in the economy, resulting in a piling up of unsold inventory. Faced with this accumulation of unsold goods, businessmen will follow the obvious path of cutting back production—that is, lower output and thus income C + S. There will be no further incentive to do so when C + I is once again equal to C + S.

Turn the whole example around. What if, for some reason, national product falls but businessmen do not change their investment plans? Then C + I will be greater than C + S, and this excess of spending over output will be noticed by businessmen as a decline in their inventories, or stockpile of goods. Business reaction to such a decline will be to raise the level of total output. Once again, the tendency to follow this course will disappear only when total spending C + I becomes just large enough to buy the total output C + S. This, to repeat, is the equilibrium level of national income or national product.

The reader may recall with memories hopefully not too unhappy, that this was done verbally, then geometrically using diagrams, and finally using some simple arithmetic.

The equilibrium discussed above will change if people alter their level of consumption and hence saving, or if businessmen change their investment plans. More consumption or more investment means pumping new spending into the economy, thus raising the equilibrium point. But less consumption (hence more saving) or less investment will lower the equilibrium.

To this point in the summary, nothing at all has been said about full employment, inflation, or depression, and this is significant. For all these labels are dependent on the size of the national income and product. If income and product are very low, there will not be enough production taking place to provide everyone with a job. At some higher point full employment will occur. While at yet higher levels, where there cannot be any further real production because the factors of production are already fully employed, any increase in national income must be due to inflation in the level of prices.

The Keynesian theory tells us that equilibrium national income occurs where total spending equals total output, but note that this can be *any* national income where that equality holds. In short, there is no automatic device which guarantees permanent noninflationary full employment.

Equilibrium can be at a low level, giving a depression; or at an overly high level bringing inflation; or just by chance, it might occur right at the level of income and output that will provide for noninflationary full employment.

At this juncture, government may be added to the picture, with the suggestion that governments spend and thus add to the economy while at the same time they tax, or subtract from it. Manipulation of government spending and taxation, called fiscal policy, has an important role in the New Economics in the elimination of inflation and depression. Adding government spending, total spending becomes $C + I + G$ (with the G being government expenditure). And with government present, total output and hence incomes earned can again be looked at in terms of how households dispose of their income, and that now becomes $C + S + Gt$ (the Gt is government taxation). Using our former logic, the condition for equilibrium is now $C + I + G = C + S + Gt$.

Government can add to total spending, and thus raise the equilibrium level of income, by raising its own spending. Or it can cut taxes and leave more available for private consumption and investment.

It can remove spending directly by reducing its own expenditure, or indirectly by raising taxes and thus discouraging private consumption and investment. That is, as stated earlier, how FISCAL POLICY works.

Before considering fiscal policy further, note must be taken that there is another method of controlling the economy, which largely antedates the New Economics but remains in constant use today. That is MONETARY POLICY, or the control of the money supply to influence the level of total spending in an economy. The idea is a simple one, although its effect is somewhat indirect. The greater the supply or stock of money in an economy, the lower its price (that is, the rate of interest). Low interest rates may encourage new investment by businessmen, thus raising $C + I + G$ and giving a new equilibrium level of national income. This would be the policy followed during a depression. The converse, lowering the supply of money in an inflationary period, may raise interest rates and discourage investment, giving a lower equilibrium for national income.

Monetary policy is managed by the Federal Reserve System in this country, and although three devices were discussed by which the Fed can exercise control over the supply of money, only one is of great importance, and that is open market operations. Of the other two, changes in the reserve requirement are seldom used, while altering the so-called discount rate has little in the way of actual impact on the money supply.

Open market operations involve the Fed in the sale or purchase of US government securities. During inflation, the Fed will want to reduce the supply of money, and thus it sells securities on the open market. People must pay the Fed for these, and they do so by reducing their bank deposits. As deposits are money, the Fed can reduce the nation's money supply (and vice-versa). The main problem is that in a depression, the Fed can create more bank deposits by open market operations, but it cannot force businessmen to invest money. Businessmen may very well not want to do so if their expectations are of poor prospects in the future.

Returning to fiscal policy, federal taxes and federal spending are subject to alteration as part of economic management. Perhaps the main difficulties here are that in time of inflation, congress and the president find that they do not gain many votes by raising taxes, and they shy away from that move. Whereas if inflation is fought by cutting spending, then it is found that many cuttable items are protected by powerful political interests, with unprotected items in the budget often of great value for a stable society. So just where can major cuts be made?

During depression, on the other hand, the danger is that increased spending of the sort that provides more grants for welfare, veterans, and so forth is difficult to cut back when the depression ends. The alternative, public works measures, takes a long time to plan and to implement.

In both depression and inflation, the New Economist is likely to run afoul of those who feel that the federal budget should always be in balance, with government spending equal to the revenue collected by taxation. But this cuts the heart out of fiscal policy, as that policy points toward the desirability of running a deficit in depression and a surplus in inflation. Fortunately deficits to fight depression are not so serious as some people believe, even though they do raise the level of the national debt. That is because both the national debt and the interest payments on it are owed by the American people to the American people, and the power of taxation is always available to meet the claims. In any case, both in our own history and the history of other countries, national debts have been far larger in percentage terms without proving ruinous.

There are today several serious problems in reconciling national goals where the New Economics is concerned. Full employment, price stability, long-term growth, and equilibrium in the balance of payments can all be managed by monetary and fiscal policy, but the prescription for any one of them might cause a worsened situation among the others. For example, full employment policies might result in some inflation and a balance of payments deficit.

A full solution to this dilemma appears difficult, in spite of several interesting experiments in economic management taking place currently in the US and abroad. Most attention has focused on prices and incomes policies—including "wage and price freezes"—imposed by the government. Such policies are attempts to control inflation without causing a corresponding rise in unemployment.

These problems are fortunately not very large in comparison with the boom-and-bust business cycle which afflicted unfettered capitalism from its earliest times in the days of Adam Smith until it was ultimately rescued by the theories of Lord Keynes and his followers.